LEGENDS *of* FAITH

Famous PREACHERS *and* EVANGELISTS

Marilyn Boyer

First printing: June 2025

Master Books, P.O. Box 726, Green Forest, AR 72638

Master Books® is a division of the New Leaf Publishing Group, LLC.

ISBN: 978-1-68344-401-5
ISBN: 978-1-61458-939-6 (digital)
Library of Congress Control Number: 2025938473

Cover: Diana Bogardus
Interior: Terry White

Please consider requesting that a copy of this volume be purchased by your local library system.

Printed in the United States of America

Visit our website for other great titles: www.masterbooks.com

For information regarding promotional opportunities, please contact the publicity department at pr@nlpg.com.

Master Books®
A Division of New Leaf Publishing Group
www.masterbooks.com

Table of Contents

Introduction 5

1. John Wesley — His Parish Was the World 11
2. Jonathan Edwards — Inspired by a Spider 23
3. George Whitefield — Voice of the Great Awakening 37
4. Francis Asbury — Circuit-Riding Preacher 53
5. Peter Cartwright — Pioneer Preacher 67
6. George Müller — Man of Prayer 79
7. Charles Spurgeon — Prince of Preachers 95
8. William Booth — General of the Salvation Army 107
9. Dwight L. Moody — Devoted Evangelist 121
10. John Harper — Hero of the *Titanic* 137

Timeline 149

Glossary 167

Corresponding Curriculum 171

Endnotes 172

Image Credits

Images created using Shutterstock AI.

Maps: *Map Trek,* pages 6, 11, 23, 37, 53, 67, 79, 95, 107, 121, 137

Introduction

In this book you will learn of 10 famous preachers and **evangelists**. They were all used powerfully by God to spread the gospel of Jesus Christ to a lost world. They came from various **denominations**, but all had one essential thing in common: they did not waver on the **fundamental** principles of the gospel.

evangelists: Preachers who often travel to share the gospel

denominations: A distinct religious body identified by traits such as a common name, structure, leadership, and doctrine.

fundamental: Basic, central

Through the years and generations since Jesus Christ died and rose again, God preserved the blessed message of the gospel. Before Jesus ascended to heaven, He gave His final instructions to His followers. "And Jesus came and spake unto them, saying, All power is given unto me in heaven and in earth. Go ye therefore, and teach all nations, baptizing them in the name of the Father, and of the Son, and of the Holy Ghost: Teaching them to observe all

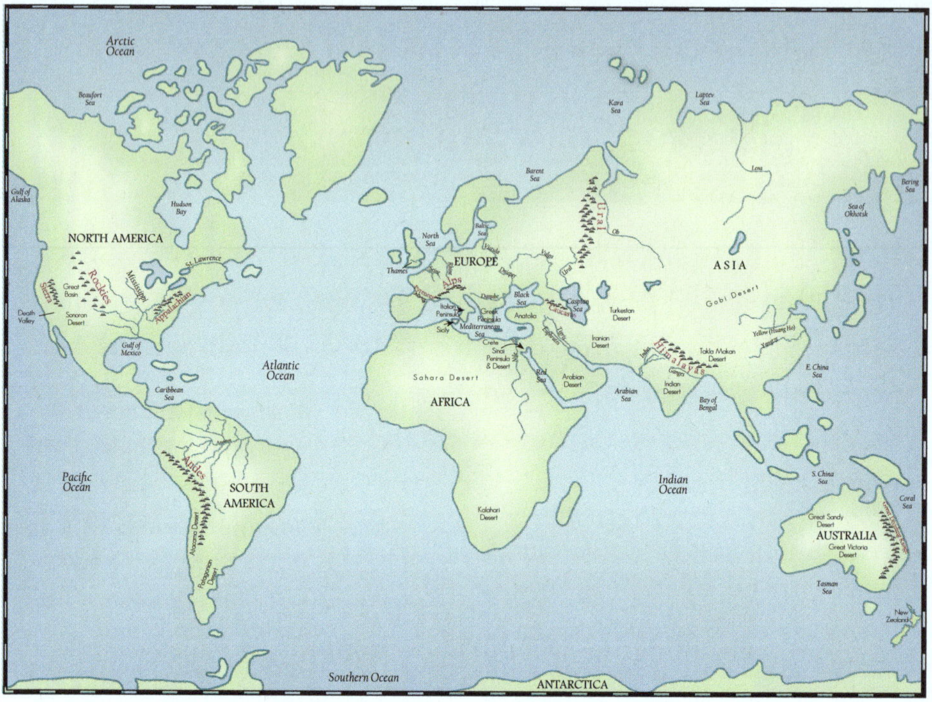

things whatsoever I have commanded you: and, lo, I am with you always, even unto the end of the world. Amen." (Matthew 28:18-20, KJV)

John 3:16 **encapsulates** the message. "For God so loved the world, that He gave His only begotten Son, that whoever believes in Him shall not perish, but have eternal life (NASB 1995)." Even though Jesus never sinned, God treated Him as if He were guilty of every sin committed by any person who would ever believe on His name. Jesus willingly died in our place. He took the penalty (suffering or loss imposed in response to a crime or offense) for our sin by His death on the cross. Jesus bore our sins so we could bear His righteousness and be allowed to enter His holy heaven. We are given the privilege to serve Him with our lives; or

encapsulates: expresses the essential features of

as 2 Corinthians 5:21 tells us, "He (God) made Him (Jesus) who knew no sin to *be sin* on our behalf, so that we might become the righteousness of God in Him (NASB 1995)."

Although the men in this book did not always agree on every point of doctrine, they did agree on this life-giving message. For instance, some believed in **Calvinism**, some **Arminianism.** Some believed in infant baptism and others in the **immersion** of the believer. Sometimes they were at odds with others who believed differently but, in the end, God used all these men to carry His gospel to the ends of the earth. There are some things we will not know until we get to heaven. What we must be clear on is how we get to heaven.

Calvinism: the belief that God predetermines who will be saved

Arminianism: the belief that affirms human free will regarding salvation

immersion: submersion in water

George Whitefield and John Wesley had some strong disagreements about points of doctrine during their lives but reconciled with the following conclusion, best summed up by a statement John

Wesley made in 1770 while speaking at George Whitefield's memorial service. Wesley praised Whitefield's admirable qualities while acknowledging the two men's differences: "There are many doctrines of a less essential nature … In these we may think and let think; we may 'agree to disagree.' But, meantime, let us hold fast the essentials …"[1]

Their mutual respect was illustrated when someone asked Whitefield if he thought he would see Wesley in heaven. Whitefield replied, "I fear not, for he will be so near the eternal throne and we at such a distance, we shall hardly get sight of him."[2]

It is truly amazing to see the **ingenuity** displayed by God as He uses man created in His image to accomplish His purposes on earth. It is encouraging to see how God directed their paths. Proverbs 16:9 tells us, "A man's heart deviseth his way, but the LORD directeth his steps"(KJV). We have much to learn from these men about prayer, dedication, and sacrifice. May you, the reader, be inspired

ingenuity: the skill and imagination to create new things

to commit your life to serving our living Savior. He wants to use your life to bring honor and glory to His name, just as He did these heroes of the faith.

1

John Wesley

His Parish Was the World

1703–1791

“I felt I did trust in Christ, Christ alone, for salvation; and an assurance was given me that He had taken away my sins, even mine, and saved me from the law of sin and death.”

Epworth, England – Born in 1703, Wesley grew up in a strong Anglican home where his mother, Susanna Wesley, played a key role in his education and faith.

Oxford, England – Studied at Oxford University and formed the "Holy Club," which laid the foundation for the Methodist movement.

Bristol, England – Preached in open-air meetings, marking the beginning of his evangelical ministry.

London, England – Established the Methodist movement and built Wesley's Chapel, which remains a key historical site. There, he passed away in 1791 at the age of 87.

Who Was John Wesley?

An English preacher and evangelist, John Wesley was used by God to convict his nation of its sin and lead people to faith in the gospel of Jesus Christ. He traveled over a quarter of a million miles on his horse, preaching 42,000 sermons, often at outdoor meetings. He led a congregation of his own as well, and his ministry impacted multiple other congregations in England and even in America. He was the author of 232 books. He is known as the father of the Methodist denomination.

Early Years

John Wesley was born on June 17, 1703, to Samuel and Susanna Wesley. Samuel was a fiery preacher, and Susanna was devoted to training her children in the **admonition** of the Lord. As soon as her children could talk, she began having them memorize large portions of Scripture. On their fifth birthday, she started teaching them to read from the Bible. She taught her children from nine in the morning until five in the evening. They were allowed a two-hour lunch break. Susanna had given birth to 14 children by the time John was born, although some died in infancy. When John was only five years old, his

admonition: teaching and instruction

family suffered a house fire that destroyed their home and almost killed John.

Plucked from the Burning Fire

John's sister Hetty awoke when a burning timber landed at the foot of her bed. She quickly woke her parents, who began leading the children safely outside. However, as the fire raged, they noticed that five-year-old John was not with them. Samuel attempted to run back into the flaming house, but the flames prevented him from entering. A neighbor spotted little John, who had woken up and gone to the bedroom window crying for help. No ladders were available. The neighborhood men stood on each other's shoulders until, finally, one man was able to snatch little John and hoist him safely to the ground. John rejoined his family. Samuel exclaimed, "This boy is a brand plucked from the burning fire! Let us give thanks to God. He has given me my eight children. Let the house go. I am rich enough."[3]

John always attributed his rescue to the Hand of **Providence** and felt God had special plans for his life.

Providence: reference to God working in our lives

The next morning, Samuel realized that he, his pregnant wife, and eight children, aged one to 17, were homeless and penniless. The children were divided up among family members and willing church members until the family was able to get on their feet again. It took a full year for the Wesleys to be reunited under one roof.

Off to School

When John was 11, his parents sent him to the Charterhouse School in London. John soon gained a reputation for being a hard-working student. He was offered a scholarship at Christ Church, part of Oxford, when he was 17 years old. John stayed at Oxford after graduation to pursue a master's degree. About this time, he started to have questions about his spiritual condition. Attempting to pursue holiness, he set up a system of strict disciplines to follow. He felt this would gain him favor with God.

After he graduated, John was ordained by the church and began preaching. He had not yet placed his faith in Christ. He later explained, "Preaching was defective and useless from 1725-1729. I neither laid the foundation of repentance nor of preaching the gospel, taking it all for granted that all to whom I preached were believers, and that many of them needed no repentance. I saw a little fruit. But—it was only a little—and no wonder; for I did not preach faith in the blood of the **covenant.**"[4]

covenant: a spiritual agreement or contract

Overseeing the Students

John received a letter in October 1729 requesting that he accept a position at Lincoln College to oversee the spiritual condition of its students. He accepted, and here he found his brother Charles had started what became known as "The Holy Club" at Christ Church. There were only three members at the time. They devoted themselves to studying the Bible on Sunday nights. John eagerly became their leader and set up rules to help the men evaluate their behavior and their spiritual heart condition. Soon, they met twice a week to study the Bible from six to nine o'clock. They

began the sessions by praying together before using the Greek New Testament to search the Scriptures. Membership in the club grew. Someone started calling them Methodists. John explained that to be called a "Methodist" meant "one that lives according to the method laid down in the Bible."[5] They decided to fast twice a week, devoting themselves to prayer. They also reached out to those in need and visited prisoners. They invited George Whitefield to join their club, which he was happy to do. During this time, George found new life in Christ. The Holy Club was the beginning of the Methodist Church which would soon spread to America.

Mission to America

John met James Oglethorpe, founder of the British colony of Georgia in America. Oglethorpe appealed to him to come to Georgia, a settlement desperately in need of spiritual teaching. He recruited several men to go with him, including his brother Charles. John made sure the men followed strict disciplines on the trip, studying the Bible earnestly. After arriving safely, John assumed his mission would be to bring the gospel to Native Americans. Instead, he was directed to minister to the English settlers. He preached his first sermon instructing the **parishioners** in the strict disciplines they must follow. Such rigid rules were not accepted well in the colony, and he was not well-liked. He became discouraged and soon headed back to England. He felt that he had failed in America. However, God, in His Providence, was about to open the door of salvation to John. He later said, "I, who went to America to convert others, was never myself converted."[6]

parishioners: church members

wrestled: deeply considered

Moravian: a member of the Moravian Church, one of the oldest Christian denominations

John Becomes a Christian

John met Peter Bohler, a **Moravian** minister who was headed to preach in America. He challenged John about his salvation, claiming that a man is saved by the grace of God and nothing else. John **wrestled** with the thought. He attended a meeting on Aldersgate Street one evening and listened as the preacher was reading from Martin Luther's preface to the Book of Romans. As Bohler began to describe the change God works in a person's heart through faith in Christ, John was moved. "I felt my heart strangely warmed. I felt I did trust in Christ, Christ alone, for salvation; and an assurance was given me that He had taken away my sins, even mine, and saved me from the law of sin and death."[7]

From that time forward, John preached the message, "By grace you are saved through faith."[8] The Church of England was not pleased with this radical message. By the end of the year, he was allowed only to preach in three or four pulpits of the Church of England. However, small Methodist societies began springing up, some led by men who had been members of the Holy Club. One night they were joined by George Whitefield. They all prayed and sang well into the night. Whitefield wrote of this night, "We continued in fasting and prayer until 3 o'clock, and then parted with the conviction that God wants to do great things among us."[9]

Preaching to the Crowds

The Church of England finally **forbade** Wesley to preach in their parishes. He explained, "God in Scripture commands me according to my power to instruct the ignorant, reform the wicked, confirm the virtuous. Man forbids me to do this in another's parish; that is in effect, to do it at all, seeing I have no parish of my own, nor probably ever shall. Whom then shall I hear: God or man? I look upon the world as my parish. Thus far… it is my **bounden** duty to declare unto all that are willing to hear the glad tidings of salvation."[10]

forbade: not allowed to do something

bounden: bound to a promise or principle

Wesley began preaching in the open air, as Whitefield had done. He preached approximately 400 sermons in six months. He and Charles preached between London and Bristol to extremely large crowds. Lives were changed. God's Word was proclaimed to all. John wrote in his journal about the transformation of the people in Kingswood, an area known for its extreme vileness: "The scene is already changed. Kingswood does not now, as a year ago, resound with cursing and blasphemy. It is no more filled with drunkenness and uncleanness and the idle diversions that lead thereto. It is no longer full of wars and fightings, of clamour and bitterness, of wrath and envyings … Hardly is their voice heard in the streets; or indeed in their own wood; unless when they are at their usual evening diversion—singing praise unto God their Savior."[11] The gospel was changing lives.

Methodist Constitution

John decided he must write a constitution to govern the Methodist societies that were springing up. He wrote rules for how men and women should act if they wished to be considered Methodists. The number of people wanting to become Methodists grew, as did opposition to the movement. Mobs formed to pelt Methodist preachers with rotten eggs, slop fed to hogs, and rotten vegetables.

John began traveling to encourage the preachers. One mob threatened to kill him. John boldly stood on a chair in the middle of the town and called out to the mob. "What evil have I done? Which of you all have I wronged in word or deed?"[12] He continued preaching for 15 minutes and ended with a prayer. When he finished, one of the leaders of the mob came forward, moved by John's words. He said, "Sir, I will spend my life for you. Follow me and not one soul here shall touch a hair of your head."[13] Seven others stepped forward also, promising to protect him.

Helper to the People

John was involved in many projects to bring relief to ordinary people. He established an orphanage in Newcastle. He opened a clinic where poor people could get appointments with a doctor and receive proper medicines. He wrote a book on health to help make people's lives better. He traveled on horseback to distribute his book. He helped to open a school for miners' children. He was instrumental in opening a school for the sons of Methodist preachers to help raise the next generation of preachers. In 1746, he set up a fund to give loans to poor Methodists. He helped 225 people in the first 18 months. In 1747, John began a ministry to Ireland.

In 1763, John began writing what eventually was called *Large Minutes*, a document outlining Methodist beliefs and practices that served as a standard for years to come. Every Methodist preacher received a copy as a guide for conducting himself in society. John, now 61 years old, loaded documents into his saddlebags again and set out on horseback to distribute them throughout England. The trip was strenuous. Although he was getting old, he still rode about 3000 miles per year, preaching more than 800 sermons.

John sent two **itinerate** Methodist preachers to America to organize Methodist societies there. One of the men he sent was Francis Asbury, who had come from a lower-class family in England. John was thrilled to see the first Sunday school organized for children in 1769. Hannah Ball, one of John's followers, started a school for children to teach reading, writing, arithmetic, and Bible knowledge. John strongly believed every child should learn to read so all children could read the Bible for themselves.

itinerate: traveling minister

How could John Wesley write so many books while traveling and preaching? John knew the country roads of England by heart. Even as an old man, John often read a book, wrote letters, or scratched down sermon notes while riding his horse at an easy pace. He trusted his faithful mount to know the way. He took good care of his horse each night and insisted that his fellow ministers do the same. John was well paid for the sale of his books but always lived a simple lifestyle. Although

he often earned 1400 pounds a year, he kept only 30 pounds and gifted the rest to Methodist charities. When questioned why he did not keep more for himself, he replied, "Money never stays with me: it would burn me if it did. I throw it out of my hands as soon as possible, lest it should find a way into my heart."[14]

John Presses On

In August 1773, John took a trip to America and preached to 32,000 people, the largest audience he ever had. John traveled and preached until a ripe old age. On his 87th birthday, he wrote about his physical decline over the last year. "My eyes were so dim that no glasses would help me. My strength likewise quite **forsook** me and probably will not return in this world. But I feel no pain from head to foot; only it seems nature is exhausted and, humanly speaking, will sink more and more till 'the weary springs of life stand still at last.' "[15]

forsook: something left or abandoned

John was often sick with coughs and colds during the winter of 1791. On March 1, he asked for a pen and paper but did not have the strength to write. The following day, leaders of the Methodist church came to his bedside. John lifted his arms skyward and pronounced a blessing on them. "Lift up your heads, O ye gates, and be ye lift up, ye everlasting doors; that this heir of glory shall come in."[16] Those were his last words. Tens of thousands of mourners came to pay their last respects to this leader of men. John Wesley shared the gospel of Christ with millions and was the father of a movement that spread God's love and the message of holy living around the globe.

2

Jonathan Edwards

Inspired by a Spider

1450 1500 1550 1600

1703–1758

"I will travel lightly through life following the footprints of God wherever they lead. For I know that He will walk beside me on the way."

East Windsor, Connecticut Colony
Born in 1703 into a devout Puritan family.

Northampton, Massachusetts – Served as a pastor and became a leading figure in the First Great Awakening, preaching his famous sermon "Sinners in the Hands of an Angry God."

Stockbridge, Massachusetts – Spent later years ministering to Native Americans and writing theological works.

Princeton, New Jersey – Became president of Princeton University (then the College of New Jersey) but died in 1758 from a smallpox inoculation.

Who Was Jonathan Edwards?

theologian: one who studies and teaches about God

Puritan: English Protestants of the 16th and 17th centuries who sought to purify the existing church

Jonathan Edwards was a preacher who helped to ignite the spiritual awakening throughout the colonies in America that became known as the First Great Awakening. His writings inspired many to seek and learn to grow in their relationship with God. He was a deep thinker and loved to meditate on God and His Word. He is known as America's most prominent **theologian.**

Early Years

Jonathan Edwards was born on October 5, 1703, in East Windsor, Connecticut. At the time, Connecticut was still a British colony ruled by England. He was born during the end of what is known as the **Puritan** era. His father and grandfather were both Puritan preachers, and Jonathan grew up knowing he would become a preacher too. He was the youngest child, the only boy in the family, and had 10 sisters. His parents taught their children at home, along with some neighborhood children. They learned to read, write, and do arithmetic. His parents prayed that their son "might be filled with the Holy Spirit; from a child know the Holy Scriptures; and be great in the sight of the Lord."[17]

When Jonathan was nine years old, he prayed five times a day. He and his buddies built a prayer

booth in the swamp near his house. The boy loved nature and felt closer to God when outside. He had worked for weeks cutting down logs and using mud, grass, and water to **chink** the cracks. He even carved a wooden cross to hang in the booth. He would pray in his booth, write in his prayer journal, and read his Bible.

chink: fill in spaces between logs

Jonathan Devotes His Life to the Lord

Jonathan loved observing every creature he could find — beetles, lizards, caterpillars, and spiders. Spiders were a great fascination. He wanted to learn how they built their webs and how they glided through the air. He did many experiments with them, making him think about how good God is to us all. Once, he held a stick as he watched a spider weave its web with a silver string produced from its tail. He began to sketch it and years later, wrote a paper about it that became known as the "Spider Letter."

Jonathan and his father often stayed up late at night talking about God around the family fireplace. One night, after the family had gone to bed, Jonathan stayed awake to read his Bible by candlelight. He gazed at his sketch of the spider's web he had drawn that day. He thought about Job 8:13-14. "So are the paths of all who forget God; And the hope of the hypocrite shall perish, Whose confidence shall be cut off, And whose trust is a spider's web."[18] As he lay there, he contemplated how quickly he had

been able to destroy the spider's carefully made web with one tiny pebble. He thought about how his parents had warned him that worldly pleasures are fleeting and do not last. He decided the time had come. He needed something stronger than a spider's web-type of faith to lean on. He needed God to be Lord of his life. That night, he placed his trust in Jesus Christ and vowed to serve Him all his life. "I will travel lightly through life following the footprints of God wherever they lead. For I know that He will walk beside me on the way."[19]

Off to School

Jonathan entered college at Wethersfield when he turned 13. He was younger than most of the other students, but he could read and write and had learned Latin and Greek. At the end of two years, he graduated and entered another branch of the school in New Haven, Connecticut, now known as Yale University. The primary aim of the college was to train godly ministers and promote the welfare of New England's churches. He spent much time in the library studying. He enjoyed all his classes. He tried to apply things he was learning to the truths he knew to be contained in God's Holy Word. He graduated at age 18, first in his class, and was offered the position of minister to a New York congregation. He later wrote,

"I went to New York City to preach, and my longings after God and holiness were much increased. I felt in me a burning desire to be in every thing a complete Christian; and conformed to the blessed image of Christ."[20]

Called to Northampton

In 1727, Jonathan was asked to assist his grandfather, Samuel Stoddard, with his duties as pastor of the Northampton congregation. Here, he married Sarah Pierrepont, whom he had met and befriended while a student. Sarah shared Jonathan's love for nature and the Lord. Jonathan was charmed by her cheerfulness. "She will sometimes go about from place to place singing sweetly and seems to be always full of joy."[21]

Jonathan was dedicated to preaching. He was concerned that the young people listened to sermons but did not change their worldly lifestyles. That all changed on October 29, 1727. That night, a catastrophic earthquake crumbled buildings in the town; aftershocks occurred for nine days. People were terrified,

including the rowdy students. They hurried to attend services and, at Edward's urging, repented of sins. Then surprisingly, not just the young people but older folks too became deeply interested in learning more about God. Edwards marveled, "God has seemed to have gone out of His usual way in the quickness of His work. It is wonderful that persons should be so suddenly and yet so greatly changed."[22]

God blessed Jonathan and Sarah with a baby. In all, they had three sons and eight daughters. They dearly loved their children and devoted time each evening to teach them the Word of God. All of Jonathan and Sarah's 11 children lived to serve the Lord. During this time, Edwards studied and prayed for 13 hours a day, taking a break each afternoon to be in the woods or outside in nature. He often rode his horse to a nearby orchard to think and meditate. He would write down thoughts and pin them to his clothing. When he returned home, Sarah would remove the pins and help him organize his recorded thoughts.

Jonathan Edwards constantly prayed for a revival in the hearts of

his listeners. One morning at church, a balcony collapsed, falling on 70 people. Thankfully, none were killed, but all were keenly aware of God's hand of protection. A revival began in Northampton and lasted for about a year. It spread to surrounding towns. Five years later, the Great Awakening occurred and continued for two years. George Whitefield was also instrumental in this revival. The two men, although different in their preaching style, respected each other and worked together.

Famous Sermon

On July 8, 1741, Edwards preached his most famous sermon, "Sinners in the Hands of an Angry God." Edwards usually wrote down his sermons and read them without showing much emotion. In this message, he drew upon his lifelong interest in spiders and their webs. He used the imagery of the delicate threads of a spider's web, the only security a spider has, to describe the real danger of hell to the unrepentant sinner. He compared how people depending on acts of righteousness to save them was just as untrustworthy as a

spider clinging to its fragile web for safety. He had witnessed many times how a small rock could destroy a carefully made web. Many were dreadfully convicted of their sin. Edwards ended the sermon by pointing them to the Cross. "But here you are in the land of the living and in the house of God and have an opportunity to obtain salvation. Therefore, let every one that is out of Christ, now awake and fly from the wrath to come."[23] God reached many hearts that day, and many gave their lives to the Lord.

People flocked to talk with Edwards after the sermon. Suddenly, his head began to swim, and he felt like he was about to faint. He collapsed on the ground and his friends carried him to the carriage and quickly drove him back to Northampton. Jonathan awoke at home with a headache and explained that sometimes he lost consciousness from exerting himself in delivering a powerful sermon. One of his friends told him, "There is an awakening brewing in our land and never have I seen God use a sermon to convict and convert so many souls. It was indeed a miracle from God, and I know he used your words to increase

His kingdom."[24] Jonathan was grateful that his prayers to see revival were being answered.

Bringing the Gospel to the Native Americans

About this time, the French and Indian War broke out in the colonies. The Native Americans sided with the French against Great Britain. Edwards felt a great desire to carry the gospel to the Native Americans. David Brainerd had been doing that very thing for the past three years. Edwards had been acquainted with Brainerd's ministry. David arrived in Northampton, suffering from the disease of tuberculosis. This illness made it difficult to travel, preach, and even breathe. Jonathan Edward's 17-year-old daughter Jerusha nursed him in her father's home, but four months later, he died.

Edwards began editing David Brainerd's diary to get it ready for publication. He emphasized how this young man had devoted his life to preaching the gospel to the Native Americans, even when he couldn't see many results for his efforts. The book became a best seller and is still an encouragement for Christians to persevere in the work of the Lord despite difficulties.

Missionary to Native Americans

In February 1751, Edwards accepted an invitation to become the pastor of a church in the small village of Stockbridge. This town was about 40 miles west of Northampton. It had been established 15 years earlier as a mission to Native American people. The population was made up of 250 Mohicans, 60 Mohawks, and a few English people. Edwards spoke, using an interpreter named John Wauwaumpequunnaunt, who knew both English and Native American languages and was familiar with the Bible. Edwards, having grown up loving nature, used illustrations from nature to explain truths to the native peoples. He said, "God's goodness is like a river that overflows all its bounds."[25] Another illustration compared the Word of God as being "ten thousand times better than the light of the sun."[26]

Edwards moved his family to the center of town, among the tribe. His younger children became fast friends with the native children and quickly learned to speak their language. All the children loved to skate on the river or sled down the hills together.

Edwards taught the tribe's children to read English. He taught them to sing English hymns of worship because he believed music softened one's heart to the truths of the gospel. He was well-liked and soon became a trusted friend of the tribe. Edwards became involved in the local school. He encouraged the children to ask questions and to learn to think. He allowed girls to attend the school as well, which was not common at that time. Soon the Mohawks and Mohicans began giving their lives to Jesus and became members of the Stockbridge church.

The French and Indian War raged on. Stockbridge remained neutral but had to become an armed camp. Edwards decided to remain with the people. During this time, he had the opportunity to write what have become some of his most famous theological books.

A New Opportunity

In 1757, Edwards was invited to become the new president of the College of New Jersey, later known as Princeton University. It was a difficult decision for Edwards to make, and he gathered pastor friends to ask their advice. They agreed that he should accept. Edwards hated to leave the mission but finally decided God wanted him to move. When he talked with Chief Hendrick, the leader of the tribe, the chief responded by saying, "God is preparing you for something different. You are unique, Jonathan. The whole world knows it. There's no one else who has your intellect, your genius. There's no one else who has your passion for holiness. And like the water that travels above the landscape, God is leading you to another city so you may tell them about the One who washes us with His grace."[27] In late January, Jonathan Edwards preached his final sermon to his church at Stockbridge. "We have no continuing city, therefore, let us seek one to come."[28] He had no idea at the time how that truth would be played out in his own life.

On to Princeton

Jonathan moved first, as Sarah had to prepare before they could move the family. He was excited to see the library of over 1200 books at his disposal. Here his family would be safe, he thought, from the

looming war with England. He was excited to have the opportunity to train young men to serve God and arm them with truth to face the challenges of life. He also would have a significant increase in income, which would be a great boost to his family. The college gave him a warm welcome, and he was anxious to get started.

The deadly disease of smallpox was spreading throughout the region. Edwards had heard of newly developed inoculations that were being tested. It was different from modern vaccinations in that it was done by injecting some of the live virus into a person's arm. Normally, it gave the person a small case of the disease which forced their body to build up antibodies to fight it. His daughter Lucy had been very ill with smallpox before his arrival and survived. On February 23, only one week after his installation as college president, he decided to take advantage of the new idea. The doctor came, made a cut in his arm, and injected pus from a diseased patient into his arm. As expected, he contracted the disease, but unexpectedly, his body was too weak to fight it off. The fever got worse, he got sicker, and his daughter Lucy was called to his bedside. He asked her to write down a message he wished to communicate with his wife and children who had not arrived in town. He grew weaker but surprised everyone by mustering the strength to say, "Trust in God, and ye need not fear."[29] These were the last words he ever spoke. Jonathan Edwards died on March 22, 1758, at the age of 55.

Jonathan had once told Sarah, "The way to heaven is ascending like a spider's web that is caught in the wind. We must be content to travel as pilgrims, uphill, though it is hard and tiresome. But going to heaven is infinitely better than the most pleasant accommodations on earth."[30] Jonathan Edwards was now in the hands of his loving heavenly Father.

Jonathan Edwards died, but his legacy lived on for many years. 173 years after their marriage, Jonathan and Sarah's 11 children produced 13 college presidents, 65 professors, 100 lawyers, a dean of an outstanding law school, a dean of a medical school, 30 judges, 56 doctors, 80 holders of public office, three U.S. senators, three mayors of American cities, three governors, one U.S. Vice President, and one senior executive in the U.S. Treasury. In addition, his descendants wrote 125 books, edited 18 journals and periodicals, and 100, following in his footsteps, became missionaries!

3

George Whitefield

Voice of the Great Awakening

“*I now began to pray and sing psalms thrice every day, besides morning and evening, and to fast every Friday, and receive the Sacrament at a parish church near the college.*”

Gloucester, England – Born in 1714, Whitefield was drawn to faith while studying at Oxford.

Oxford, England – Became part of the Holy Club alongside John and Charles Wesley.

London, England – Preached to large crowds and helped expand the evangelical movement.

American Colonies – Made several missionary trips, becoming a key figure in the Great Awakening, preaching in Georgia, Pennsylvania, and Massachusetts.

Newburyport, Massachusetts – Died in 1770 and was buried at Old South Church.

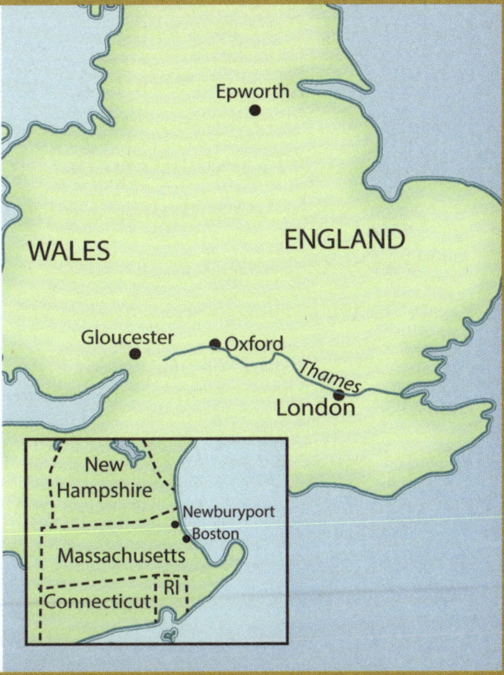

Who Was George Whitefield?

Blessed with a booming voice that carried to crowds of thousands of people, George Whitefield spent his life reaching the hearts of his listeners for the gospel of Jesus Christ. His goal was to preach to as many people as possible, including slaves, Native Americans, orphans, poor people, and the rich alike. God used this young preacher in America, Scotland, and England. He preached his first sermon at age 23 and throughout his lifetime spoke to millions of people, preaching more than 18,000 times.

Early Years

George Whitefield was born on December 16, 1714, in Gloucester, England. His parents owned a prosperous inn in the center of town. When George was only two years old, his father died suddenly. His father had managed the thriving business; now, the family had to scramble to fulfill his responsibilities. After a couple of years, the inn began to decline. George's older brothers stepped up to take on much of the work. However, of all her children, George's mother had chosen him to receive a higher education. She perceived he was very bright. She instilled in young George a sense that God would use his life. Often, the inn was used by traveling actors to perform plays. George loved listening to them and imitating the lines. He was drawn to public speaking as well. His family attended church services each week, after which George would entertain family and friends by acting out sermons and devotional readings he had heard.

A Flair for Public Speaking

Flair: able to do something very well

grammar school: school that taught languages and basic math and geography

By the time George was 12 years old, his acting and speaking talents were known at school as well. He entered St. Mary de Crypt, a **grammar school** in Gloucester. Acting and public speaking became his passion. He studied how an actor should convey emotion through facial expressions and body movements. George had to leave school early when the family finances were no longer adequate for his schooling. He moved into a small house with his mother, but he felt in his heart that God would deliver him from the difficult circumstances. He confided in his sister, "God intends something for me which we know not of. As I have been diligent in business, I believe many would gladly have me for an apprentice, but every way seems barred up, so that I think God will provide for me some way or other that we cannot comprehend."[31]

The Answer Comes

Very soon after, a young student and former schoolmate came to rent a room from George's mother. He told George he was working his way through Pembroke College at Oxford University as a servitor. A servitor's job was to be a personal servant to one of the wealthy students. His duties included shining a student's shoes, cleaning his room, running errands, washing his clothes, and waking him up in the morning. In exchange for his help with everyday tasks, his expenses were covered, and he was able to study for his degree. George and his mother were excited about the opportunity. George had plenty of experience waiting on others at the inn. He was not afraid of hard work. He spent the next two years finishing up his education at St. Mary de Crypt at their parish church. George began to take his spiritual life more seriously. He decided that he wanted to be a minister. As of this time, he did not know Jesus Christ as Savior.

A Devoted Life

Whitefield chose not to participate in worldly pleasures with fellow students. Instead, he set a new set of disciplines for himself. "I now began to pray and sing psalms thrice every day, besides morning and evening, and to fast every Friday, and receive the **Sacrament** at a parish church near the college."[32] George often isolated himself to study more. His disciplined lifestyle was noticed by all.

Sacrament: a religious act done with reverence and obedience

methodically: systematically

athirst: being eager, urgent need for something

In the summer of 1733, Charles Wesley invited him to breakfast. Whitefield had heard of a small group of men known as the "Holy Club" or "Methodists." They were called this because they **methodically** established spiritual routines to follow. He was amazed that Charles would invite him, a servitor, but he was pleased to go. "I thankfully embraced the opportunity; and blessed be God! It was one of the most profitable visits I ever made in my life. My soul, at that time, was **athirst** for some spiritual friends to lift up my hands when they hung down, and to strengthen my feeble knees."[33]

Charles explained, "My brother John and I have noticed your faithful attendance at church, and we've heard about the good works you have been doing. We felt we needed to see you face-to-face."[34] When breakfast was over, George left carrying the first of many books Charles would lend him. George soon became known as one of those "Methodists" in the Holy Club. Other students made fun of George, but he continued to devote himself to God and to visiting the sick and poor.

Trying to Please God

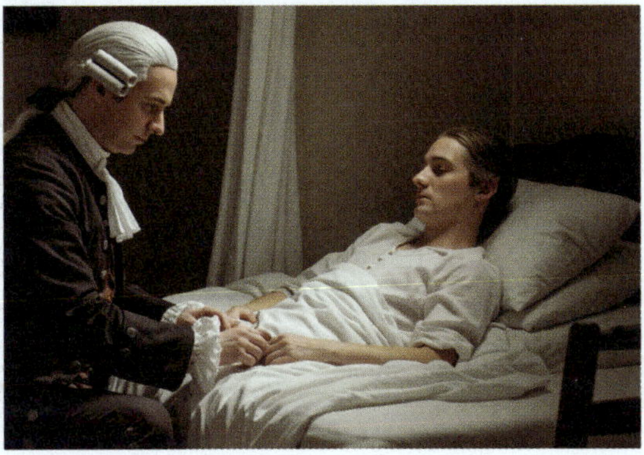

George began to carry his spiritual discipline to an extreme. He denied himself proper food to the point that he became deathly weak and sick. A doctor was called and confined George to bed for seven weeks. He had tried as hard as he could to get closer to God, but he felt no closer. Alone in his bed, he bowed his head and threw himself on God's mercy. He finally realized that the Lord Jesus had saved him, George Whitefield, and all who believed on His name when He died upon the Cross. Jesus had paid the penalty for his sin. His salvation was not dependent on the good things George had tried to do. George always spoke of this day as the most important day of his life. He often spoke of it in sermons. Having discovered new life in Jesus Christ, he would, from now on, devote his entire life to shouting the good news to the ends of the earth!

George Whitefield — Preacher

On June 20, 1736, George Whitefield was **ordained** as a deacon at Gloucester Cathedral. That afternoon, he read prayers to prisoners. Seven days later, he preached his first official sermon as an ordained minister in St. Mary's de Crypt, the church he had attended as a boy. The church was packed with people curious to hear this young man preach his first sermon. George thought only of the message God had laid on his heart. When he was done, a hush fell over the congregation. He had a way of holding listeners spellbound. At the end of

ordained: officially made

June, George returned to Oxford to receive his bachelor's degree and begin graduate studies. He was now leader of the Holy Club, as the Wesley brothers had left for America as missionaries.

In August, George received a request to come to London to preach at the chapel of the Tower of London. He spent two months there, and the response to his preaching was overwhelming. He prayed, "Awake this city to you, Lord Jesus."[35] People from all walks of life flocked to hear him preach: soldiers, the rich, and the desperately poor. Bible stories came alive as he told them with his dramatic flair. The chapel was overflowing every Sunday.

More Opportunities

After being back at Oxford for only two months, George again received a request to fill in for a minister who was taking classes. This time, it was at a small country church full of very poor folks. George was eager to accept the opportunity. He was welcomed and shown respect by all in the community. People, many of whom could not read, flocked to hear him. He explained the Bible to grandmothers, farm workers, children — all who would listen. His listeners were so appreciative. One farmer told him, "Can't none of us read a word, Reverend, and when we hear you read the Bible, it's just like God writes it on our hearts."[36] George felt it just as much a privilege to preach to these receptive hearts as to preach to the great and rich members of society.

Turning England Upside Down

Charles Wesley had been writing to George, begging him to make a trip to the colony of Georgia in America. Georgia was the newest colony and was home to many poor people. George was happy to go. He would have to return to England in a year or two for his **ordination** ceremony. The governor of the colony of Georgia, General Oglethorpe, was in England at the time on business. He invited George to travel with him to Georgia after a month or so. While waiting, George continued preaching to crowds that grew larger each time he spoke. While preaching in Bristol, the head of the prison came to hear him, got saved,

ordination: to be officially recognized as a representative of the Church

and invited George to preach to the prisoners and pray with them each morning. The jailer began immediately establishing reforms to make the prisoners more comfortable. God had transformed his life. The prison had been known for its filth and cruelty, but no more.

Oglethorpe was delayed, so George used the time to preach in London and Bristol. People were leaving their churches to listen to Whitefield. Many church leaders were not happy, however. It was said, "Whitefield upsets all of England. He sounds like a Puritan with all his talk about sin and holy living. Such preaching has no place in the Church of England."[37]

His preaching was appreciated by Lady Huntingdon, a member of the royal family, who was a follower of the Methodist teachings herself. She gave her time and resources to aid Methodist ministers and provide an outlet for them to be heard. She often invited Whitefield and other young preachers to speak to her guests. Her guests were polite to listen, although not many appreciated the preacher's views. They did not appreciate being told they were miserable sinners. George, however, was delighted to share his message of Jesus Christ with these members of the **aristocracy**. He believed all men were sinners and needed the grace and mercy available through Jesus Christ. Just before he left for America, thousands came to hear him preach in London. Some said, "His voice is like thunder, straight to the heart, and 'tis the sweetest sound anyone has ever heard. God has raised up this man for this hour, for England."[38] And yet, God was about to broaden his ministry.

aristocracy: the highest class in certain societies

Off to America

Savannah, Georgia, was basically a clearing in the woods with about 100 makeshift cabins to house its population of 500. Counting the surrounding areas, less than 1000 people lived in Georgia. The people were extremely poor. George had wisely prepared supplies to bring. He brought, among other things, hammers, axes, clothing, nails, powder and shot, medicines, paper and quills, books, spices, oatmeal, and cheeses. Many children were left uncared for when their parents died. Some were taken to work for others as slaves. Many were poorly clothed and barely fed. General Oglethorpe had asked George to set up orphanages and schools for the children. He was eager to do so. George believed the children were the future of the colony of Georgia. He planned to give them a proper education in the Scriptures and developed a plan for shaping their character. The people were hungry for the Word of God. One farmer said, "Reverend Whitefield's the only man of God I ever heard talk so plain and easy with the likes of us."[39] George reluctantly said goodbye when the time came to return to England to be ordained, but he intended to raise money to help fund the orphanages while there. He would return.

Ordained Minister

George was ordained and used every opportunity to preach while in England. He felt he must reach out to coal miners in Kingswood. The miners lived in horrible conditions and had no

preachers to go to them. The first day he preached to the men, he had 200 listeners. The next day, he had 2000. Streaks of white made from tears streamed down many of the miner's faces as they responded to his message of hope and mercy. The final time he preached to them, 20,000 people came: miners, farmers, and townspeople. George prayed, "Give me eyes to see whatever you have sent me to use as a natural sounding board. Let the wind aid my voice, Lord, and give me wisdom to deal with those who might disturb the listeners."[40]

The Lord worked mightily through his message. He even raised more funds for the orphanage in America. His time in England was growing short, but he felt he must preach in Moorfields Park, a place where rough crowds gathered for dog fights, public hangings, picking pockets, and the like. He was told he would not come out alive. He went anyway, planning to preach on Sunday. Great crowds gathered as he stood on a stone wall to preach. As usual, George prayed for the Lord's help. The crowd grew to 30,000 people, but an observer could almost hear a pin drop as they breathlessly listened. They had never heard anyone speak with such power about the living God. Many people came to know the Lord that day as George preached about forgiveness and the new birth.

Off to America Again

George explained to the newly saved captain of the ship bound for America about his mission. An itinerate preacher may preach in churches but also speak outside in the open. He goes wherever he is led to go. George explained that the orphanage would be where he had his base of operations. From there, he would leave on preaching tours throughout the colonies. "The world is now my parish," he explained.[41] After 11 weeks at sea, they arrived.

One person who listened to George Whitefield whenever possible was Ben Franklin. He had read about large crowds listening to Whitefield in the fields of London. He conducted an experiment while Whitefield was preaching. Franklin explained, "I had the curiosity to learn how far he could be heard, by retiring backwards down the street toward the river; and I found his voice distinct till I came near Front Street, when some noise in that street obscured it. Imagining then a semicircle, of which my distance should be the radius, and that it were filled with auditors to each of whom I allowed two square feet, I computed that he might be heard by more than 30,000."[42]

After Whitefield's first visit to Philadelphia, Franklin observed, "And it was a matter of speculation to me, who was of the number, to observe the extraordinary influence of his oratory on his hearers. … It was wonderful to see the change soon made in the manners of our inhabitants. From being thoughtless or indifferent about religion, it seemed as if all the world were growing religious, so that no one could walk through the town in the evening without hearing psalms sung in different families of every street."[43]

Soon, Franklin began printing George Whitefield's sermons to be distributed. Their friendship lasted throughout their lifetimes. Franklin supported Whitefield's work in the orphanages. He contributed more than a year's salary to help support them. He also helped raise money for land and a building to be built for a church. It was used as a charity school for children during the week. The charity school later became the University of Pennsylvania.

When Whitefield reached Virginia, he was surprised to find that some men had printed his sermons and formed reading groups that met in homes. Someone would read his sermons, and many were convicted of sin and led to repentance. More groups were started. Whitefield spent some time there encouraging the believers in this work. These groups eventually became the start of the Presbyterian Church in Virginia.

Whitefield was often afflicted with illness, but it rarely kept him from riding the circuit and preaching. He was exposed to bad weather often. Sometimes he had to rest in bed to regain strength to preach, but he never gave up. He raised money to help support an Indian School in Connecticut, where Native Americans were trained to spread the gospel among their own people. His orphanage in Georgia prospered and grew.

George's Last Trip to America

In all, George Whitefield made seven voyages across the sea to America. On his final trip, great crowds gathered each time he spoke. He stopped first to see the orphanage. The initial stage of his planning was on the 5000-acre lot that had been given to him. He was pleased that the school was well underway, and new orphans were arriving continually. Next, he told his helper, Richard, that they must visit Savannah and then Philadelphia. Bursting with excitement, he said, "I feel such a fire of joy inside that it blazes up and I am ready to preach the love of our Lord Jesus wherever he leads us."[44]

In Philadelphia, crowds were so enormous that he had to preach twice on Sundays and three to four times each week. Crowds feared they would not hear him again, as news had spread that he was afflicted with spells of sickness. However, he felt strong enough to keep going. He told Richard to acquire horses so they could ride to New York. He preached all along the way. He rode over 500 miles and then turned toward Boston. He was invited to preach in the pulpit of a descendant of the great Puritan preacher Cotton Mather. Whitefield noted: "I feel as I did when I stood in the pulpit of that giant of the faith, John Bunyan. It is a privilege."[45]

The huge congregation listened spellbound. That night, Whitefield and Richard headed on to Boston. On the way, George's illness flared up again. Richard urged him to rest, but George was determined to press on. When they reached Newburyport, Massachusetts, he found a large crowd waiting for him. He mustered the strength to preach for two hours in an open field. Exhausted, he headed for bed in the minister's home. Richard slept in the same room in case George's breathing became too labored. Richard awoke during the night to the sound of George gasping for breath. The doctor was summoned, but it was too late. George breathed his last as he finally lay still, Richard having supported George's weak and failing body. It was in the early hours of September 30, 1770. As news of his death spread, England, Scotland, Wales, and America mourned his passing.

George Whitefield's Legacy

During his lifetime, George Whitefield spoke to millions of Americans, preaching over 18,000 times. He held services for slaves in the colonies and helped establish schools. He used newspapers, pamphlets, books, and even criticism from his enemies to draw attention to the gospel. It's been estimated that 80% of Americans during that time had the opportunity to hear him preach. Crowds that numbered in the tens of thousands gathered to listen to him.

Great Awakening: a religious revival that impacted the English colonies in America during the 1730s–1740s

George Whitefield's name was known throughout America. He is credited for being instrumental in the **Great Awakening** that swept through not only America but also Scotland, England, and Wales.

4

Francis Asbury

Circuit-Riding Preacher

D. 1450 1500 1550 1600 1745–1816

"*I would say, go into every house, … go into every kitchen and shop, address all, aged and young, on the salvation of their souls.*"

Hamstead Bridge, England – Born in 1745 and trained as a Methodist preacher.

America – Volunteered for missionary work in 1771 and spent the rest of his life traveling as a circuit-riding preacher, spreading Methodism across the young United States.

Spotsylvania County, Virginia Died in 1816 after establishing Methodism as a major force in America.

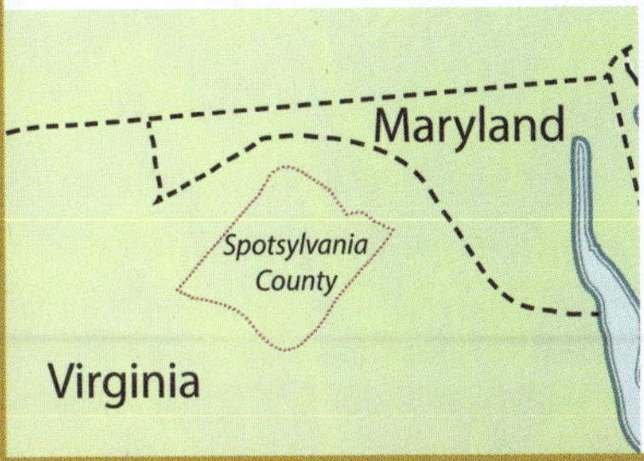

Who Was Francis Asbury?

Born in England, Francis Asbury devoted his life to preaching the gospel to anyone who would listen. He felt called to the American colonies, where he spent most of his life as a circuit-riding preacher. Preaching over 16,000 sermons, he traveled a quarter of a million miles sharing the good news of Jesus Christ with rich and poor alike. He became one of the first two bishops of the Methodist Episcopal Church in America. He was an instrumental preacher in the **Second Great Awakening**.

> **Second Great Awakening:** the revival in the United States from about 1795 to 1835 when many people turned to God

Early Years

Francis, better known as Frank, was born in 1745 in Staffordshire, England, to Joseph and Elizabeth Asbury. When Frank was just three years old, his only sister, aged five, died. His mother became terribly depressed, but through the ministry of a Methodist preacher, she was led to the Lord. From that day on, she enthusiastically began to read her Bible daily, spending hours in prayer. She encouraged young Frank to do the same. When Frank was 14 years old, he attended a meeting and heard a traveling Baptist preacher speak of God's gift of salvation. When he returned home, Frank went out to the barn, knelt, and placed his life and future in God's hands.

A Change of Plans

Frank's father **apprenticed** him to a buckle maker so the lad would have a good trade. Frank completed his apprenticeship at the age of 22 and returned home. His father and mother were proud of him for working hard to become a tradesman. His father told him that he had saved a small sum to help Frank open his own shop. Frank swallowed hard and told his father that his plans had changed. Frank had decided to become a traveling Methodist preacher. His father, not being a Christian, was outraged that his son would give up a good-paying career to roam around the countryside preaching. He knew his son had been influenced by the Wesley brothers. He pointed out that the Wesleys had a fine college education and were ordained ministers. Frank had no such education. He told Frank he would be doomed to be poor his whole life, unable to support a wife or family. Frank's mother was more understanding. Frank assured his family that he loved them dearly, but he must do what he believed God wanted him to do.

apprenticed: to learn a trade under a craftsman

Frank had been attending Methodist society meetings during his time as an apprentice. John Wesley had loaned him many books to read. He had been under the ministry of various Methodist leaders. Mr. Griffin, to whom he had been apprenticed, had allowed Frank to take Sundays off. After a time, Frank was given opportunities to preach. A group of five young men had formed to study the Bible and pray. Frank had been chosen to be the leader. They volunteered to preach over a 12-mile circuit, preaching four times on Sundays at different locations. Then he volunteered to be the local preacher, all the while keeping up with his apprenticeship duties. Yes, Frank knew this was how he must spend his life.

Circuit Riding

Early in 1766, Frank began his circuit-riding ministry, traveling on horseback. It was often dangerous. He would preach to rough groups of men, coal miners, or rich people—whoever would listen. He spent much time reading the Bible, praying, singing hymns, and preaching. He was careful to write to his parents often. He told them he would "rather be in a saddle than in a seat in the House of Lords."[46] As a Methodist circuit-riding preacher, Frank was expected to get up at 4:00 a.m. on days when he preached and 5:00 a.m. on other days. He spent the first hour of his day in prayer and the second hour reading and meditating on verses from the Word of God. He met with other Methodist leaders he encountered, and all

held each other accountable to uphold their standards of discipline. He remembered John Wesley's exhortation, "You have nothing to do but to save souls. Therefore, spend and be spent in this work. Gaining knowledge is a good thing, but saving souls is better."[47]

Frank met other preachers who had been to the American colonies and heard of the great need there. He felt God was leading him to cross the ocean and preach in the colonies.

Off to America

In September 1771, Frank and his friend Richard Wright boarded the ship bound for America. The members of the Methodist society in Bristol had taken up offerings to supply each man with a change of clothes, blankets, and 10 **pounds** each. Other than that, Frank had his Bible and some books, as well as a large pulpit Bible to be given to the Methodists in Philadelphia.

pound: a unit of money used in Britain

Frank was deathly ill with seasickness for the first four days of the journey but felt better by the fifth day. Frank and Richard took turns on Sundays preaching to the passengers and sailors, although none were converted. Finally, on October 27, the ship reached land. Frank and Richard set out to find a man named Francis Harris, whom John Wesley had contacted to host the travelers. They received a warm welcome and were given opportunities to preach in the local church, but Frank was anxious to get out on the circuit.

Hardships to Bear

It is hard to imagine the discomfort Frank faced. As he once said, "I seldom mount my horse for a ride of less distance than 20 miles on ordinary occasions; and frequently have forty or fifty in moving from one circuit to another. In traveling thus, I suffer much from hunger and cold."[48] His horseback mileage for a year generally totaled between 4000 to 6000 miles.

The harsh New England winters brought snow, ice, and wind. The clothes that the Methodist society in England had given Frank were not adequate to keep him warm. He was often sick but usually still managed to preach. Frank preached wherever his horse stopped. In his journal, he recorded, "I feel happy in speaking to all that I find, whether parents or children, or servants; I see no other way. I would say, go into every house, … go into every kitchen and shop, address all, aged and young, on the salvation of their souls."[49]

Frank suffered a severe bout of malaria and had to spend a few months recovering in the home of a devoted Methodist couple in Maryland. Upon recovery, he spent time in New Jersey and Pennsylvania, visiting and encouraging Methodist societies. Back in Maryland, at the age of 31, Frank suffered a severely ulcerated throat. He was nursed back to health by a wealthy merchant, Henry

Gough, and his family, who lived in Baltimore. Here, he learned of the signing of the Declaration of Independence.

Trouble in the Colonies

England was now at war with her colonies. The certainty of conflict spurred Frank on to pray more and work harder at preaching. He set up many Methodist societies around the countryside. He felt the burden that many men might be called up to fight and die before they found peace in their souls through salvation. He received a letter from England suggesting all Methodist preachers return to England so as not to be caught in war. He chose to stay. "North America was his mission field and that is where he would stay."[50]

The Americans had experienced defeat in Long Island. Despite dire circumstances, Frank always tried to focus people's attention on spiritual matters. He did hope the Americans would win the war but encouraged all to realize God would bring about His desired outcome.

No man could now preach in the colony of Maryland unless he took an oath to defend the colony. If they did not agree to take the oath, they were considered to be **Loyalists**. Frank, an Englishman, felt he could not take the oath. He could not take up arms because

Loyalists: loyal to England and in opposition to independence

brigades: divisions of the army

he felt compelled to spread the gospel message. Another wave of Methodist preachers left for England. Frank felt alone but secure in the belief that he was where God wanted him. Frank stayed in the home of a Methodist judge in Delaware. In this colony, preachers were not required to take the oath. Frank had written a letter to his superior in England. He wrote that he felt it would not be long before America was a free and independent country, and he felt too bound to the Americans to leave them. The letter was confiscated and came into the possession of Caesar Rodney of Delaware, one of the signers of the Declaration of Independence. Governor Rodney realized then that Frank was not a British supporter and, to Frank's delight, gave him permission to preach freely in Delaware.

The War Continues

Frank soon felt the freedom to travel to some of the other colonies as well. He often encountered **brigades** of American and British soldiers. It was common for soldiers from both sides to sneak off to hear Frank preach. Horses were in demand and could be confiscated for use in the war. Frank prayed that no one would demand his horse, and thankfully, no one did. One night, however, after having ridden past British and American troops, Frank took off his hat to find it had a bullet hole through it. He never knew which side had fired, but he was grateful for God's protection.

Frank found much poverty in the southern colonies, with few schools and fewer churches. He preached wherever anyone would listen—whether in a tiny cabin or in large spaces. He once preached in a tobacco warehouse where 500 people had squeezed inside to hear him. He usually traveled more than 20 miles a day, urging his horse to swim across rivers and leading him through briars or rocky roads. He was often afflicted with chiggers or ticks. Frequently, he slept in the woods using his saddle as a pillow. Besides all that, he was often sick from spending so much time in swampy areas.

Friendly Acquaintances

In North Carolina, he met Harry Hoosier, a black preacher whose master had freed him from slavery. Frank marveled at what a dynamic preacher he was and how God was using his message to bring salvation to many. Although he had never learned to read or write, he began attracting greater crowds than Frank. Frank praised the Lord for how Harry was able to touch the hearts of so many men and women. The state

of Indiana is now nicknamed the Hoosier State after this preacher who was used mightily by God during the Great Awakening.

In his diary regarding his travels in the south, Frank records, "Within this six months, I have traveled, according to my computation, two thousand six hundred and seventy-one miles."[51]

The War Ends

While in Culpeper, Virginia, in May 1782, Frank learned the fighting had ended. He wrote in his journal, "Here I heard the good news that Britain had acknowledged the independence for which America has been contending—may it be so! The Lord does what to Him seemeth good."[52] Eleven days later, Frank attended the Methodist conference in Baltimore, where he learned that a letter had arrived from John Wesley appointing Francis Asbury as primary leader of the Methodists in North America. After the conference, Frank again mounted his horse to ride the circuits and encourage Methodist preachers and members. In 1780, there were 42 Methodist preachers, 20 circuits, and 8,504 members. After the war, the numbers began to grow immensely. In 1784, there were 83 preachers, 46 circuits, and 15,000 members! Frank presided over it all, and it kept him quite busy.

Officially an Established Church

In December 1784, a meeting was held to officially establish the Methodist Episcopal Church. It was no longer under the authority of England but strictly American in nature. Francis Asbury was ordained as a bishop. Frank, trained as a buckle-maker, had never expected to have this honor bestowed upon him. He organized his

flock of circuit riders. They had a reputation. There was a common saying, "The weather is so bad today that nothing's out but crows and Methodist preachers."[53] It pleased Frank to know that his "cavalry of preachers" were doing their jobs.

America's First Methodist College

At a meeting of Methodists held on Christmas Day 1784, a vote was passed to establish a new college. Cokesbury College was built and opened in 1787, the first Methodist college in the United States. It was named after both Thomas Coke and Francis Asbury, the first two Methodist bishops in America. Its purpose was to train both the sons of traveling Methodist preachers and orphan boys. Rules were put in place to shape the boys into godly young men. The Methodist Episcopal Church became the first religious denomination in the

United States to officially congratulate the newly elected President George Washington and wish him well. As the country began expanding westward, settlers faced threats from attacks on the frontier. Frank insisted on sending out preachers and going himself to

encourage settlers and make sure they had men to minister to their needs. By 1790, the Methodist church had over 57,000 members and circuits in all 13 of the states as well as the frontier territories.

The Work Goes On

Frank marked his fiftieth birthday on August 20, 1795. His hair was now gray, and his body was feeling the wear and tear of strenuous travel. Still, Frank somehow managed to ride over 1000 miles every three months in all sorts of weather. At times he was so weak that he had to be strapped to his horse to keep from falling off. His circuit preachers expected him, so he pressed on. Friends on the circuit took care of him. One lady made him a new suit of clothes each year. Others prepared little **chambers** in their houses for him to lodge during his travels.

By 1802, camp meetings were springing up throughout the nation. Often, 1000 people or more gathered for three to seven days to pray, sing, and listen to preaching and teaching. The number of people giving their lives to the Lord kept increasing. As the church grew, more and more young men stepped up to become circuit riders and carry on the work. "Bishop Francis Asbury was widely thought to be the most recognized person in the United States."[54] Thousands of people claimed Frank to be their "spiritual father." As Frank grew more feeble, he sometimes had to be carried to meetings. His legs bothered him so much that he sometimes had to preach while on his knees.

chambers: guest rooms

Frank turned 70 years of age and was still traveling. He was training a young man named John Wesley Bond to take over for him. Sometimes, when Frank was too weak, he would preach from his carriage. On Sunday, March 31, 1816, Frank could go no further. He and John were staying at a friend's home in Spotsylvania, Virginia. Frank collapsed and was put to bed, but he insisted that

the family gather around him for Sunday worship. He encouraged them all by reading from Revelation 21 about the new heavens and earth when all believers would dwell together for eternity. Then Frank asked to be put in a chair. He raised both his arms toward heaven as he breathed his last.

At his memorial service, about 25,000 people gathered—black, white, young and old, highly educated, and folks who could not read. When Frank first arrived in America, the Methodist church had 600 members. Now, in 1816, it had grown to 214,000 members. 700 preachers were riding the circuits. One American in every 40 now claimed to be a Methodist. One of his circuit-riding preachers spoke at the service. "What could he do that he did not do? For he exhausted all his strength, broke down his constitution, spent his talents and his all, and wore out his life, for the good of man and for the glory of God."[55]

5

Peter Cartwright

Pioneer Preacher

1785–1872

"This camp meeting kindled a religious flame that spread all over Kentucky and through many other states."

Amherst County, Virginia
Born in 1785 and moved with his family to Kentucky.

Kentucky & Illinois –
Became a Methodist circuit-riding preacher, ministering to settlers on the frontier.

Pleasant Plains, Illinois
Died in 1872 after nearly 70 years of ministry.

Who Was Peter Cartwright?

For more than 60 years, Peter Cartwright rode on horseback throughout eastern America, preaching the gospel of Christ to everyone who would listen. He is considered a pioneer because he rode before established roads were constructed. He was one of the key preachers of the Second Great Awakening in America and personally baptized 12,000 new believers.

Early Years

Peter was born on September 1, 1785, in Amherst County, Virginia. His father fought in the War of Independence. Although his mother had grown up as an orphan, she was a godly woman and loving mother. When Peter was five years old, his family moved westward from the state of Virginia to land now in the state of Kentucky. This area was a wilderness, occupied by hostile Native American tribes. His family joined with 200 other families for mutual protection. They were also accompanied by 100 strong men, paid to protect them on their journey. All the men took turns guarding the group. One night, when it was Peter's father's turn to keep watch, he heard movement in the brush and grunting that sounded like a hog. He knew there were no hogs in this wilderness area. He decided to shoot at the object that was moving slowly toward him. Others in the camp heard the gunshot and came running. They discovered that he had shot a Native American who had been approaching him with a gun in one hand and a tomahawk in the other. His alertness had saved the settlers from disaster. They saw evidence of other pioneers who had not been so fortunate along the way. Peter, though only five, never forgot that wilderness trip.

Young Peter

Peter's mother opened their home to circuit-riding preachers throughout his childhood. In his autobiography, Peter told of a camp meeting nearby when he was about 15. Ministers of all denominations were present; approximately 15,000 people had traveled to be there. Peter explained, "This camp meeting kindled a religious flame that spread all over Kentucky and through many other states. And may I be permitted to say, that this was the first camp meeting ever held in the United States, and here our camp meetings took their rise."[56] God moved mightily, and many were saved.

Peter Becomes a Christian

Despite his mother's godly influence, Peter described himself as a wicked boy. He spent hours doing mischief, fighting, and showing off. One evening, his mother invited him to a gathering at the Presbyterian meetinghouse. A Methodist preacher named John Page was to speak. Peter immediately refused, but noting the hurt in his mother's eyes, he agreed to go with her. Several

intrigued: drawn in

hundred people attended that night. The service opened with hymn singing led by Presbyterian pastor James McGready. He then preached the first sermon of the evening. Peter had heard that this pastor led more people to the Lord than any other man in the West. As Peter listened, he found himself **intrigued** by the message. The preacher was describing that the way of sin and death was a reality, not just words. "Dark is the road that leads to death. And thousands walk together there, on that dark road … wandering, lost, doomed."[57]

Preacher McGready sat down, and John Page got up to preach. He spoke with hope as he proclaimed God's love in sending His Son to forgive sin. He explained that God promised new life to those who would follow Him wholly. Peter thought it sounded marvelous but concluded it could not be for him. Then John Page seemed to look right at Peter. "God's promise is for everyone, or it means nothing. He meant that life for you. Come forward now, all who accept God's promises, and begin the new life."[58] Peter felt himself drawn to the front of the church. There he knelt as the preacher led him to the Lord. When he arose, the congregation was singing, "O, For a Thousand Tongues," a hymn written by Charles Wesley. From that day on, this hymn had a special meaning for Peter. He wished he had a thousand tongues with which to praise God.

Peter felt as though he were seeing the world for the first time. His mother hugged him, and John Page shook his hand and invited him to join the Methodist society at Ebenezer Church. The following June, Peter was baptized.

Preacher Boy

> **laymen:** non-clergy men who had responsibilities helping with a church

Peter attended church meetings with his mother. John Page only came about every six weeks because he was riding the circuit. **Laymen** of the congregation, called "exhorters," led the other meetings. In the spring of 1802, the preacher in charge of a quarterly meeting handed Peter a paper. It said, "Peter Cartwright is hereby permitted to exercise his gifts as an exhorter in the Methodist Episcopal Church, so long as his practice is agreeable to the Gospel."[59] Peter was astonished. The preacher explained he had heard Peter giving his testimony in class meetings and stated that he was a powerful speaker. "I don't know how to preach!" Peter protested. The preacher told him he would learn by doing. He emphasized that the need for circuit riders was desperate, and exhorters made it possible for the preachers to travel and share the gospel in unreached areas.

That fall, Peter attended a meeting of the Western Conference of the Methodist Episcopal Church. He learned that there were 7,000 Methodists living west of the mountains. There were only 27 traveling preachers whose circuits covered extensive areas. Peter first met Francis Asbury at that meeting. Peter had the opportunity to escort Brother Asbury across the mountains. They formed a friendship that lasted throughout their lifetimes.

Moving West

Peter's father moved the family west again later that fall to Lewiston County, which was 80 miles away from the nearest circuit. Francis Asbury gave Peter the responsibility of traveling throughout the region, setting up a new circuit, and holding meetings. Peter felt inadequate to the task but he said, "I did the best I knew how."[60] At the annual conference, Peter reported that he managed to add 70 members to the society and set up the new circuit. He was only 18 years old at the time.

Peter was assigned to a new circuit with Ralph Lotspeich. Instead of just functioning as an exhorter, however, he was asked to preach. He tried to refuse, but Brother Lotspeich insisted. Peter began to pray. "I asked God, if he had called me to preach, to give me aid that night, and give me one soul, that is, one convert under my preachin', as evidence that I was called to this work."[61] God answered his prayer that night. One man, known for his unruliness and unbelief, was powerfully **converted** and became a wonderful Christian example for the rest of his life. Never again did Peter doubt that God wanted him to preach.

Peter Gets Married

Peter was assigned to a new circuit and began preaching at a farm in Barren County, Kentucky. Here he met Frances Gaines, the daughter of one of the exhorters in that area. Peter thought about

Frances over and over while on the circuit. He looked forward to seeing her at the next camp meeting. The couple had much in common, and Peter asked Frances to think about marrying him. He explained that the life of a circuit rider's wife was not an easy one. When he returned in a month, Frances accepted. On August 18, 1808, Frances' 18th birthday, they were married. Peter rode the circuit and Frances stayed home, did the gardening, preserved their food, and cared for the house. Their first child, Eliza, was born in 1810. During this time, Peter managed to buy a small home for his family. Two years later, baby Maria was born.

converted: saved

Francis Asbury was growing old. He felt compassion for the circuit riders who had families to support. Asbury took up a collection to present each rider with ten dollars for each of his children. Peter knew this had been a "work of love … love for all the men and above all for the church."[62]

Full-fledged Preacher

Francis Asbury was always an inspiration and encouragement to Peter. At the 1804 annual conference, Asbury was pleased with the good reports he heard about Peter. For the next 20 years, Peter would ride the circuit as a pioneer in the West. He had to travel in all types of weather, frequently sleeping on the ground using his saddlebags as a pillow to rest and sleep. He often went without food for two or three days at a time. He crossed rivers eight to ten times just while making one circuit. Peter met other circuit riders—Methodists, Baptists, and Presbyterians—all men who were tough enough to endure the **elements** and devoted enough to **persevere**. Circuit riders were supposed to be paid $80 a year but felt fortunate if they were paid half that amount.

Another War

In 1814, the news came that a mighty British fleet was sailing toward New Orleans, the major trade center for the whole Mississippi Valley. Peter joined General Andrew Jackson's army as a **chaplain**. He did his share of the work helping the soldiers to build fortifications a few miles below the city. He served alongside the men, enduring rain, bugs, and inadequate food. On Christmas Day, he preached to hundreds of soldiers. The battle took place in the Louisiana swamps. When it was over, hundreds of British were dead or wounded. The Americans lost only 13 soldiers; there were 58 casualties. Peter encouraged the wounded and was glad when all could head home. Having been off the circuit for over two months, Peter had to do much catching up. Some nights he was so tired he fell asleep in the saddle. In the spring of 1816, he was saddened to hear that his **mentor** Francis Asbury had passed away.

elements: bad weather

persevere: keep on when conditions were hard

chaplain: preacher

Meeting Andrew Jackson

One night, Peter was caught in a driving thunderstorm. He was drenched to the skin, and his horse was terrified of the blasts of lightning. He was scanning the horizon to catch a glimpse of the lights of Nashville, his destination. Instead, he came upon a large, well-lit house. He knocked on the door. Imagine his surprise when the door was opened by Andrew Jackson himself! Peter apologized, explaining that he had not recognized the house as being **The Hermitage**. General Jackson politely **bade** him enter and sit by the fire while he set out dry clothes for him. Jackson insisted Peter spend the night in one of his spare bedrooms. He told Peter he had heard a great deal about him and knew he had volunteered as a chaplain in the Battle of New Orleans. He introduced Peter to his wife Rachel who placed supper before him. The evening was spent in conversation about political affairs. Peter agreed with many of Jackson's ideas. Jackson told Peter he would make a good politician. Peter told General Jackson that he would make a fine Christian. Jackson threw back his head and laughed. He replied, "Fair enough, preacher. But I'll bet you'll be in politics long before my name's on any church roll."[63] Jackson was not a Christian, but Peter could not help liking the man.

mentor: advisor

bade: asked

The Hermitage: the name of Jackson's home

Peter Becomes a Legislator

Peter relocated his family to Illinois. A year before he moved, there had been a strong campaign within the state legislature to permit slavery. Peter joined the anti-slavery group. He had always been against the practice and made it a priority to preach to all people, black as well as white. Before long, he was asked to run for a seat in the legislature. Cartwright agreed because he felt so strongly that slavery was wrong. He was elected to two terms as representative from Sangamon County.

In 1832, Peter met Abraham Lincoln when he ran against him for Congress. Lincoln was elected; Cartwright defeated. Years later, Cartwright defended Lincoln. He explained losing to Lincoln: "I went down to defeat, but it was defeat by a gentleman and a patriot."[64]

Peter was not ashamed to speak out for what he believed. While in office, he introduced several bills. One was to prohibit saloons within a mile of a camp meeting or a college of learning. Another bill concerned the fair distribution of funds to schools. He wanted to protect state banks and **seminary** lands, and he wanted to see a state university established. It was due to his efforts that the Illinois State Historical Society was organized. He served on many important committees. Education was a priority for Peter.

seminary: colleges for preachers

Last Conference

At the yearly conference of 1869, Peter decided it was time to announce his retirement. The secretary at the conference reported that Peter had served eight years in the Tennessee Conference, four years in the Kentucky Conference, and 45 years in the Illinois Conference. Peter was now 84 years of age, the oldest active itinerate preacher. Peter gave a speech expressing thankfulness for 65 years of service to God as a minister. In that time he baptized 15,000 children and adults and brought 12,000 people into the church. He had preached two or three times a day for 20 years as a young preacher. During his last years, he preached four sermons a week. He estimated that he preached over 16,000 sermons in all. He expressed appreciation for a wife who supported his ministry, raised eight children, and worked on the farm when he was absent. He had 50 grandchildren and 37 great-grandchildren. He said if he had to do it all over again, he would choose the life he had lived rather than be President of the United States. Peter asked people to pray that God would continue to use him during his last years in some capacity. People flocked forward, recalling specific instances of how his preaching had influenced and changed the course of their lives for the glory of God.

While riding home on the train, he led some people in his favorite hymn, "O, for a Thousand Tongues to Sing My Great Redeemer's Praise." Peter thought about the night almost 70 years ago when he had been converted. He had wished for a thousand tongues to praise God. Now Peter Cartwright realized his wish had come true. "He had a thousand tongues, a hundred thousand tongues—the tongues of all those people whose lives he had touched and changed. And they in turn spread the praise of God to others, to their children and grandchildren, in a chorus which would continue as long as the world existed, and the church survived. He sang with all the joy of that vision:

'My gracious Master
and my God,

Assist me to proclaim,

To spread through all
the earth abroad,

The honors of the
Name.'" [65]

Peter continued to minister to people until on September 25, 1872, God quietly took the 87-year-old preacher home.

6

George Müller

Man of Prayer

1805–1898

“*The greatness of the sum affords me a kind of secret joy; for the greater the difficulty to be overcome, the more will it be seen to the glory of God how much can be done by prayer and faith.*”

Kroppenstedt, Prussia (Germany) – Born in 1805 and later converted to Christianity after a reckless youth.

Bristol, England – Founded the Ashley Down Orphanage and became known for his deep faith and reliance on prayer for financial provision.

Bristol, England – Died in 1898, leaving a legacy of faith and charity.

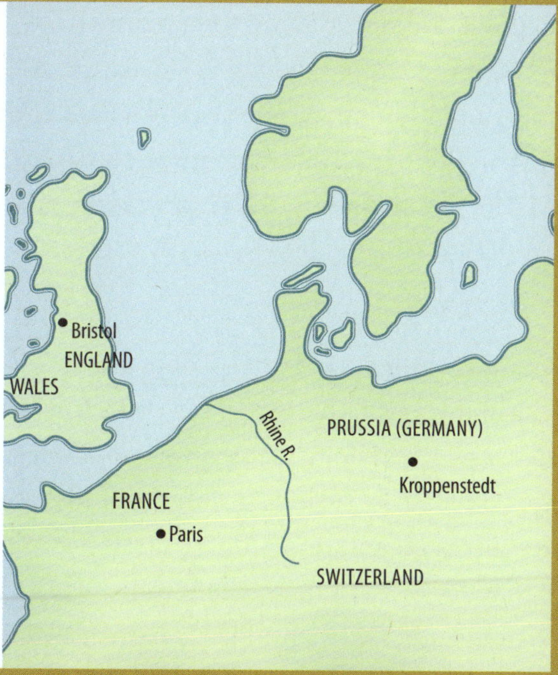

Who Was George Müller?

George Müller was a man committed to the power of prayer. He had a rare, extraordinary trust for God's provision that is still an inspiration today. Müller was a Christian evangelist who opened orphanages in Bristol, England. He cared for 10,024 orphans in his lifetime and never asked for a penny from anyone but prayed to the Lord to supply their every need. He not only gave the orphans food and lodging, but he also provided education and spiritual instruction. The children witnessed God's daily provision and Mr. Müller's deep faith in the God who provides.

Early Years

George Müller was born on September 25, 1805, in Kroppenstedt, Germany. His father was a tax collector; his mother died when he was 14 years old. George was not honest as a child. When he was only 10, he began stealing from his father and friends. He was arrested and imprisoned, but this did not stop his wicked behavior. In 1815 he was sent to the Cathedral Classical School in Halberstadt, Germany, for his early training.

The Lutheran church was the official state church in **Prussia,** an area in the country of Germany. Pastors were paid well and were respected members of the community. When George graduated from classical school, his father enrolled him at Halle University. This school prepared men for the ministry. George was happy to go. He wanted to obtain a job sufficient to meet his financial needs. He realized that when he graduated, his father would no longer pay his bills. He began to develop quite a reputation for partying and **carousing**. He realized he needed to change his ways. However, his resolve did not last long. George was the life of every party and entertained folks with his wild stories. One night, a new but familiar-looking student showed up. He had been a fellow student at the Cathedral Classical School. His name was Beta. He had been serious-minded and refused to join in wild entertainment. He always carried his Bible around and prayed a lot.

Prussia: today's modern Germany

carousing: enjoying oneself in a noisy, lively way

Herr: German word for Mister

George Becomes a Christian

One night Beta invited George to attend a meeting with him. George reluctantly went along. **Herr** Wagner warmly welcomed George and Beta into his home. Soon hymnbooks were distributed, and the group began singing. George thought the people sang as if they were singing about someone they knew. After singing, Herr Wagner fell to his knees and led the group in prayer. George had never seen a person kneeling to pray. When he finished, Herr Wagner opened his Bible and read a chapter. Then he started his sermon. George slowly became interested. After an hour and a half, Herr Wagner prayed in a way George had never heard before.

It sounded as if Herr Wagner were talking to a friend in the room. It seemed like he meant every word he said. George sat stunned. On the way back to their rooms, Beta asked what George had thought of the meeting. He told Beta nothing he had ever done had been as enjoyable as that meeting. Beta invited him back the next night and the next. Before a week was over, George was kneeling by his bed confessing his sin to the Lord and committing his life to Jesus.

Friends began to see a drastic change in George's behavior. He stopped going to parties and gambling and drinking. All he wanted to do now was read his Bible, talk about God, and head off to those nightly meetings to hear the sermons. After six weeks, George made a remarkable decision: He would dedicate his life to being a missionary. When he told his father about his decision, Herr Müller became angry. He decided he would no longer support his son. He felt as if the money he had invested in George's training would be a waste since missionaries did not have a way to obtain a good living. George was on his own to provide for his education in the missionary training school.

Need for Money

George had never had to provide for himself. He did not know what to do. He fell to his knees and began to pray. Shortly after, there was a knock on his door. Dr. Tholuck, Halle University's new Professor of Divinity, stood there, along with three professors visiting from Princeton University in America. Dr. Halle offered George a job tutoring these three men in German. George spoke English as fluently as his first language. George would tutor the three men for eight hours a week. They each agreed to pay twice the normal rate for tutoring. This meant George would be paid six times the amount a tutor is normally paid. Dr. Tholuck also told George there was a room available at the Franke Orphanage across the street. It had only been an hour and a half since George had prayed. He got on his knees again, this time giving thanks to the God who answers prayer.

Franke Orphanage

George learned that Dr. Franke, the founder of the orphanage, had been a professor of theology at Halle University a hundred years ago. He had felt called to help the poor orphans in town. He did not have much money but somehow managed to feed, clothe, house, and educate 2,000 orphan children.

The orphanage was still functioning with no regular source of income. Dr. Franke had written in his will that one room in the orphanage would be reserved for a deserving theology student to use free of charge. George was chosen to be that student. George marveled at the great faith it must have taken Dr. Franke to be responsible for the welfare of so many children.

George Müller began to have opportunities to preach. His first sermon was to be given at a small country church. George had worked long hours to polish his presentation and delivery. It did not go very well. Some of the parishioners told him they had not understood a word he said. As a result, he concluded that from then on, he would preach using simple, understandable words, quoting only from the Bible. He was scheduled to preach again that evening. He spent the afternoon on his knees in prayer and chose to preach from the fifth chapter of Matthew. The sermon was received with smiles. One lady told him he had made the Bible come alive for her. George had learned a lesson he would never forget.

Ebenezer Chapel

George suffered some health problems, and his doctor suggested that he go to the seaside to escape the smog of the city. He settled on Teignmouth, a fishing village in southern England. While there he met a Scotsman named Henry Craik. Henry was George's age, and like George, had become a Christian during his college years. From Craik, George learned about a man named Anthony Groves, who had sold all he owned to become a missionary. His story fascinated George.

Henry arranged for George to preach at various chapels in the area. Twelve weeks later, Ebenezer Chapel extended a call for George to become their pastor. The congregation was mostly fishermen and their wives. George accepted.

While there, he also traveled to surrounding towns and held meetings. When visiting Exeter, he met Mary Groves, a sister of missionary Anthony Groves. She was a strong Christian woman. The more time George spent with her, the more he liked her. They were married on October 7, 1830.

Depending on the Lord

George became convinced that he and Mary should shed the **encumbrances** of earthly goods such as Mary's silver and fine dishes. This would allow them the freedom to travel and relocate as God led them. He also told his congregation they would no longer collect **pew** rents, a customary amount preachers charged their members for a seat on a pew. The richer members paid more for seats near the front of the chapel. The poor people had to settle for the "cheap" seats. This rent helped to pay the preachers' salaries. Up till this time, Ebenezer Chapel had been paying George 55 pounds. George felt emphatically they should depend only on God for their needs. He felt members should give freely, not under compulsion. George and Mary hung a box in the church and told the members they would never ask for money. No longer would they collect pew rentals. After hanging the box, George and Mary knelt by a pew and prayed for God to provide for them.

encumbrances: burdensome possessions

pew: long wooden rows used as seats in church

Things did not always seem to go smoothly. On one occasion, George and Mary sat down for dinner with empty plates before them. George began to lead in prayer when there was a knock at the door. They opened the door, and a friend handed them a ham. Another time, a stranger knocked on their door and extended a freshly baked loaf of bread. As the year ended, George reflected on what he and Mary had learned: First, God did provide their needs. They had never missed a meal. Second, they had learned much about trusting God. They had given away extra money to others in need. George had given up a salary of 55 pounds, but by the end of the year, he had been blessed with almost three times that amount. The church had grown in membership, and George and Mary were expecting their first child.

Moving to Bristol

Henry Craik invited George to visit him in Bristol, a populous, bustling port city in southwest England. George and Henry held 10 days of meetings at Gideon Chapel, where Henry pastored. People swarmed to listen; many had to be turned away for lack of room. Members of Gideon Chapel begged George to move to Bristol. George and Henry agreed to be joint pastors to share in the work. George went home to relocate his family to Bristol.

Soon after the Müllers moved, there was a cholera outbreak in Bristol. Cholera was a bacterial infection that caused severe diarrhea and vomiting. Often, it took only 12 hours before the infected person **succumbed**. It spread like wildfire. Thousands of people in Bristol died. George and Henry ministered to the sick, holding the hands of the dying and reading Scripture to them. The church members decided to keep meeting to pray. By the time the epidemic was over, only one member of the congregation of 200 had died.

succumbed: died

After the epidemic ended, George became burdened by the number of children who had been orphaned because of the disease. They often had no one to care for them and wandered the streets begging for food.

The Breakfast Club

George and Mary started what they called "The Breakfast Club," opening their home to serve breakfast to orphans in the city. They read to the children from the Bible. Within a month, they were serving 20 to 30 children daily. The number soon grew to 40. George realized they could no longer fit in his small house. He prayed continuously about the problem, and an idea began to develop in his mind. He wanted to start an orphanage.

Müller held a public meeting to explain his idea. He stated that there would be no asking for money—he would rely on God's provision to meet the many needs of the orphans. The orphans would be schooled, fed, and housed. Some women volunteered to help care for the orphans. Other people handed him money. One

couple came to offer their services to help run the orphanage. Many gave furniture, tableware, bedding, clothes, and supplies. George kept careful records of all the donations. He found a house for rent, and soon the money was supplied to pay for it.

The Orphanage

On February 3, 1836, the orphanage at 6 Wilson Street opened its doors. It had only been seven weeks since George had held the public meeting in Gideon Chapel. By the end of the month, George had 26 girls, with 42 more on the waiting list. A local doctor offered to treat sick children for no charge. Before long, there were more orphans than George could fit in the house. In October, he rented another house on Wilson Street. This building would house babies and toddlers. Many of the girls from the first orphanage helped to care for the babies. Next, George opened a boys' orphanage which accommodated 40 boys.

George continued praying. Orphans kept coming. Soon, he had 150 children who depended on him for food and clothes every day.

He was still co-pastor at Gideon Chapel, distributing Bibles to people who could not pay for them. One day, he received complaints from neighbors on Wilson Street. The orphanages were noisy. The street drains that handled sewage often clogged up from overuse. George knew something had to be done, and as always, he resorted to prayer.

Ashley Down

George discussed the problem with his daughter Lydia. She said she wished he could buy a large piece of land to build new buildings for the children. George began to pray again. "So, God, I put it right in your hands. I need to find about seven acres here in Bristol, on a hill if possible. Then I need a contractor to build a place for 300 children. And I need 10,000 pounds."[66] This was his prayer for 36 days. On December 10, 1845, he received 1000 pounds. This was a start.

Mary's sister came from London for a visit. She told George she knew a contractor who agreed to construct the building and supply his labor for free. Donations came in bit by bit. In February, he heard about land for sale at a place called Ashley Down. It was seven acres, with fields and plenty of space for the children to play. The air was fresh and clean, refreshed by breezes from the nearby sea. George went to see the owner of the land. They agreed he would return the next day to discuss the price. The following day, the owner told him he had not been able to sleep all night. God

had impressed upon him that he should sell the land to George at a greatly reduced amount. George now had the land and the contractor. In six months, he accumulated 11,000 pounds in the building fund. Construction began on July 5, 1847. The home was ready for children two years later. Three hundred orphans walked from Wilson Street to their new brick home on Ashley Down.

George kept praying. Orphans kept coming. A second house on Ashley Down was built six years later. Whenever needs arose, George fell on his knees, and funds began to trickle in. The orphans were witnesses to God's miraculous provision. At one point, George had 300 children sit at the table for breakfast with empty plates in front of each. He assured the children that God would provide. They all bowed their heads in prayer to thank God for what He would give them to eat. Suddenly, they heard a knock at the door. There stood a baker with a huge tray of freshly baked bread. "Mr. Müller, I couldn't sleep last night.

I kept thinking that somehow you would need bread in the morning and that I was supposed to get up and bake it for you. So, I got up at two o'clock and made three batches for you. I hope you can use it."[67] Just a few minutes later, there was another knock at the door. The milkman explained that the wheel on his cart had broken just outside the door of the orphanage. He needed to lighten his load before he could fix it. George had 20 of the older children help carry the 10 large milk cans to the kitchen. This was enough for each child to have a glass, and there was even enough left over for lunch.

God Provides

Time and again, the children saw the Lord provide. There were times when there was no money to pay daily expenses. Every time George prayed, just enough money would come in to cover daily costs. Most people would be afraid to trust in God to provide large sums. Not George Müller.

"The greatness of the sum affords me a kind of secret joy; for the greater the difficulty to be overcome, the more will it be seen to the glory of God how much can be done by prayer and faith."[68]

George often said, "Showing Christians that God is able to answer prayer was one of the reasons I decided to build the orphanage at Ashley Down."[69] In 1870, the fifth house was built. A month later, Mary grew sick with rheumatic fever. It was the first time she had been sick in years. On February 6, 1870, Mary went to be with the Lord. Two thousand orphans came to honor her at the funeral. George and Mary had been like parents to the orphans.

George now spent even more time with the orphans. Some who had grown up, left, married, and started their own homes returned

to visit. They wanted to introduce their children to the man who was the "beloved father of the orphans." On March 9, 1898, George, now 92, worked at the orphanage but began to feel overly tired. That evening, he led the prayer meeting for the orphans before retiring. He read his Bible, went to sleep, and died peacefully in his bed at 5:00 the following morning. Fifteen hundred orphans and thousands of people attended his funeral, the largest Bristol had ever seen. In 63 years, George Müller cared for over 10,000 orphans. In his lifetime, one and a half million pounds had passed through his hands to others. In addition to caring for the orphans, he printed and distributed Bibles, started and supported Sunday schools, and even sent Hudson Taylor enough money to support all the missionaries of the China Inland Mission!

The work of George Müller's orphanages continued after his death. More than 17,000 orphans were cared for at Ashley Down until the 1950s. The orphanages were closed after that, but the Müller charities changed form and are still active today. They contribute over one million pounds to disadvantaged children and families at home and abroad.

7

Charles Spurgeon

Prince of Preachers

1834–1892

"Those preachers whose voices were clear and mighty for truth during life continue to preach in their graves."

Kelvedon, Essex, England – Born in 1834 and converted to Christianity as a teenager.

London, England – Became the pastor of the Metropolitan Tabernacle and one of the most influential Baptist preachers of all time.

Menton, France – Moved there for health reasons and passed away in 1892.

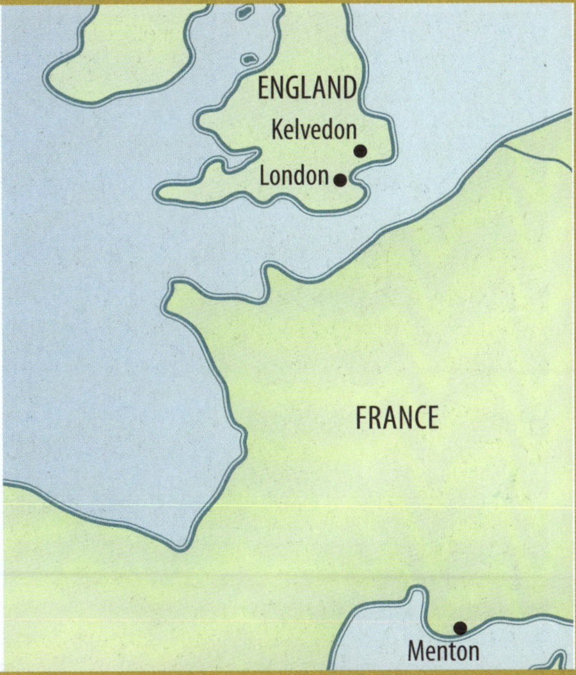

Who Was Charles Spurgeon?

Charles Haddon Spurgeon was the pastor of the Metropolitan Tabernacle in London for 38 years. His sermons held his listeners spellbound and were transcribed, translated into many languages, and widely distributed. He authored many commentaries, devotionals, books on prayer, and even an autobiography. His sermons were used by God to draw sinners to Jesus Christ who died for their sins. A month before he died, he said, "Those preachers whose voices were clear and mighty for truth during life continue to preach in their graves."[70] This has certainly been true for Charles Spurgeon, the man known as the "Prince of Preachers." By the time he died he had preached to millions of people and baptized thousands. His books are still read and quoted by pastors today.

Early Years

Charles Haddon Spurgeon was born on June 19, 1834, in the village of Kelvedon in Essex, England. Charles was the first of 17 children born to John and Eliza. His father was a Congregationalist preacher. Charles learned to preach sermons as a young boy. He watched his father prepare to preach and spent many hours with his grandfather, who was also a preacher. When he was seven years old, he gathered his brothers and sisters in the barn, climbed into the hayrack, and enthusiastically preached to his siblings and the cows. He learned from this experience. As a man, he once taught students, "You do not thoroughly know any truth till you can put it before a child so that he can see it."[71]

Charles spent summers with his grandparents for several years. While he was there and wanted to earn some extra money, his grandmother promised him a penny for every hymn he memorized. He learned so many that she finally had to cut the payment in half. Charles never forgot those hymns and often quoted them in his sermons.

Spurgeon loved nature. Once at his grandparents' house he saw an apple inside a bottle. The apple was almost as wide as the bottle, and he was puzzled as to how it got inside. His grandmother explained that she placed a small apple in the bottle while it was growing and waited until the apple grew before removing the bottle. Later in life, Spurgeon used this illustration to show the value of teaching children about Jesus while they were still very young.

Charles was schooled in his early years by a tutor from whom he learned French, Latin, and Greek. At age 14, he studied at an agricultural school. The next school he attended was New Market Academy, where he was asked to tutor younger students. He memorized long passages from Puritan sermons and sections of John Bunyan's *Grace Abounding to the Chief of Sinners*. He recited them to his fellow students.

Charles Is Saved

Despite his knowledge of the Bible, young Charles often wondered how God could really love him. It troubled him that he could never obey like he wanted to no matter how hard he tried. One terribly snowy Sunday, his father was preaching in a small town 12 miles away. He did not take his family with him as was his custom because of the heavy snow. Charles attempted to walk to a church in town. The snowstorm grew heavier, and he stumbled upon a small church he had never visited before. Taking refuge from the storm inside, he noticed how few people were in attendance. The preacher had not even been able to attend because of heavy snow.

A layman stood up and **expounded** on Isaiah 45:22, "Look unto me, and be ye saved, all the ends of the earth (KJV)."[72] He looked into Charles' eyes and said, "Young man, you look very miserable. And you will always be miserable, miserable in life and miserable in death, if you don't obey my text. But if you obey now, this moment you will be saved. Young man, look to Jesus Christ! Look! Look! Look! You have nothing to do but to look and live."[73]

Spurgeon later told the story, "I saw at once the way of salvation. Oh, how I did leap for joy at that moment. I looked until I could have almost looked my eyes away, and in heaven I will look still in my joy unutterable."[74] His mother noticed a definite change in her son in the days ahead. He seemed joyful and studied his Bible every chance he had.

expounded: commented

Spurgeon Preaches

Spurgeon was offered a job teaching in a school in Cambridge. He taught so clearly that even adults came to hear him. When a small church in nearby Teversham needed a preacher, one of the pastors at Cambridge thought of Spurgeon. He knew Spurgeon would not feel he was ready to preach, so he asked him to attend the church as companion to a young man who would be preaching. Charles accepted but found out along the way that the same pastor had asked his companion to accompany Charles who would be preaching. Someone had to preach, so Charles agreed. The people

loved his preaching. He continued preaching during the week in homes or even barns.

In 1851, he preached at a small church in Waterbeach, in Cambridge, England. The congregation asked him to be their pastor. He preached there for two years, although he was only 17 years old. During this time, the congregation grew from 50 to 400 people. The gospel was changing lives. People were giving up their bad habits and spending time in Bible study.

Preaching in London

One Sunday in 1853, Charles received a letter asking him to preach at New Park Street Chapel in London. It was a well-known church that had been pastored by many famous men. At first, Spurgeon thought the letter was meant for someone else, as he was only 19 years old. On December 17, he traveled to London, a city with a population of three million people. He chose James 1:17 as his text: "Every good gift and every perfect gift is from above, and cometh down from the Father of lights, with whom is no variableness, neither shadow of turning (KJV)." The church could seat 1200 people but had dwindled in size to only 40 in recent years. Spurgeon, as usual, spoke a simple message of God's love for sinners. It was like a breath of fresh air compared to sermons the people were used to hearing. That night more people came to hear him. The church officials asked him to preach for three more Sundays. When the time was up, they sent him a letter offering him the permanent position of pastor. He accepted ten days later, on April 29. Before long there were 1800 people regularly attending the New Park Street Chapel. The church overflowed and some gathered around the windows to listen. By June 1856, the deacons rented Exeter Hall, a larger building, but by October, Exeter Hall was overflowing. Hundreds of people had to be turned away each Sunday. Next, they rented the music hall in the Royal Surrey Gardens. This hall had a seating capacity of 12,000.

Spurgeon Marries

In 1854, Charles met a young lady in his church whose name was Susanna Thomson. Susanna was impressed with how Charles spoke with such simplicity that anyone could understand and yet still addressed the deepest needs of the human heart. Charles' first gift to Susanna was a copy of *The Pilgrim's Progress* by John Bunyan. Charles had read it over 100 times. Charles and Susanna were

commentaries: books that help explain the text

unfailing: reliable

amplify: increase the volume

married on January 8, 1856. The following September, Susanna gave birth to twin boys, Charles and Thomas. Susanna often helped Charles prepare to preach by reading aloud to him from **commentaries**. Charles explained, "I am glad to call my dear wife to my assistance. She reads to me until I get a clear idea of the whole subject."[75] Susanna was a constant encouragement to her husband throughout their marriage and was a loving mother to their children. She taught them to read and understand the Bible. Susanna would often play hymns on the piano while singing with the boys. Spurgeon was not paid a high salary. Susanna wrote, "Many moving tales could we tell of anxious hearts and an apparently **unfailing** purse in those first years of trial, but always, yes, always our God put our fears to flight and sent the needed funds to us, sometimes from an utterly unexpected quarter."[76]

In 1857, Spurgeon was preparing to preach at Crystal Palace, a huge building made of metal and glass. It had been constructed to house the World's Fair of 1851. He and his helpers were trying to decide where to place the pulpit so that more people could hear his voice as there were no microphones to **amplify** the sound. To test the best arrangement, Spurgeon shouted the words from John 1:29: "Behold the Lamb of God, which taketh away the sin of the world (KJV)." A worker in one of the galleries did not know anything about the test. To him, it sounded as if a voice from heaven was addressing him. He shared many years later that those words brought him to salvation in Jesus Christ.

Somehow, even though funds were scarce, the couple managed to help pay college fees for a young man who desired to become a pastor. This gave Spurgeon the idea of building a college to train young men to be pastors. He wanted a school they could more easily afford. He raised funds, and the college opened that same year. They called it the Pastors' College. During Spurgeon's lifetime, 853 men graduated from the college, including his two sons.

The Metropolitan Tabernacle

In 1861, construction was completed on the Metropolitan Tabernacle. It had been built specifically as Spurgeon's church. It accommodated 5000 people and was the largest church building at that time. Spurgeon preached there for the next 31 years. He began to have his sermons transcribed and printed and distributed all over the country. He also printed Bibles to give away. He spoke to his students at the Pastor's College every Friday. His message was always, "Preach Christ, always and evermore. He is the whole gospel.... The world needs still to be told of its Savior, and of the way to reach Him."[77] Many of his teachings were made into a book entitled, *Lectures to My Students*. Susanna thought the book was so helpful that she began a project collecting money to have it printed so it could be distributed to pastors who could not afford to pay for it.

The Tabernacle was open daily to assist any members of the community who needed help. A widow donated some money to Spurgeon. He used the money to build an orphanage for boys. He also built one for girls 10 years later. The orphanage was designed to house the children in small groups so that each child received close attention from a lady who acted as a mother to them. Spurgeon visited the children often. The children were taught about Jesus and given an education to prepare them to be able to get jobs when they grew up. He also started many schools for poor children in London. Spurgeon wrote many books. He was one of the best-selling authors of the nineteenth century. He wrote a seven-volume set called *Treasury of David*, which is still considered the best devotional commentary of the Psalms ever written. He donated income from book sales to fund his many projects.

Spurgeon's Last Sermon

Spurgeon had been battling health problems for many years. On June 7, 1891, he preached at the Tabernacle, exhorting his congregation to place their trust in Christ. "These forty years and more have I served Him, blessed be His name, and I have nothing but love from Him. I would be glad to continue yet another forty years in the same dear service here below if so it pleased Him. His service is life, peace, joy."[78] This was the last of over 3000 sermons he had preached in that church. The doctor sent him to Menton, France, a seaside town, to escape the smog of London. His health continued to deteriorate and on January 31, he died at age 57. His last words to Susanna were, "Oh wifey, I have had such a blessed time with my Lord. My work is done. I fought the good fight. I have finished my course. I have kept the faith."[79]

One writer noted that when [Spurgeon] preached "He preached to the masses, and he preached to each listening individual. He preached to royalty, and he preached to orphans. He preached to minds, and he preached to hearts. History will forever know Charles Haddon Spurgeon as the Prince of Preachers."[80]

8

William Booth

General of the Salvation Army

A.D. 1550 1600 1650 1700

1829–1912

"... while there remains one dark soul without the light of God, I'll fight—I'll fight to the very end."

Nottingham, England – Born in 1829 and experienced a conversion to Christianity as a teenager.

London, England – Founded The Salvation Army in 1865 to minister to the poor and bring the gospel to those in need.

London, England – Died in 1912, leaving behind a worldwide movement of Christian charity.

Who Was William Booth?

William Booth was an English Methodist preacher. Burdened by the poverty and suffering he saw in London, England, he was motivated to preach in the open air to multitudes of people. The misery he saw led him to start The Christian Mission, which later became known as The Salvation Army. His intention was to point as many people to salvation as possible. He lived to be 83 years old, preaching more than 60,000 sermons over that lifespan. He traveled more than five million miles, establishing and maintaining chapters of The Salvation Army. In the last sermon he ever preached, he declared, "While women weep as they do now, I'll fight; while little children go hungry as they do now, I'll fight; while men go to prison, in and out, in and out, I'll fight; while there remains one dark soul without the light of God, I'll fight—I'll fight to the very end."[81]

Early Years

William Booth was born on April 10, 1829, in Nottingham, England. William's father was a successful builder. Unfortunately, hard times came, and he could not sell the homes he had built. Eventually, he failed to pay the mortgage on his family's home and could not afford to keep William in school. Mr. Booth then apprenticed 13-year-old William to a **pawnbroker**. William lived with the pawnbroker in a poverty-laden section of Nottingham called Goose Gate.

pawnbroker: a person who lends money at interest

Many people who could not afford rent lived on the streets, struggling to obtain food and clothing. The pawnbroking business was simple. People brought in items to sell. The pawnbroker noted the value of each item and then paid the customer about sixty percent of its worth. He held on to the items for two weeks in case the customer found a way to reclaim them. If not, the pawnbroker sold the items and profited forty percent.

Some men pawned the tools of their trade to put food on the table. Willam wondered how they would ever get back on their feet this way.

A few months later, William's father died. William wanted to help support his mother and sisters, so he sent what little he made home to them, but it was not enough. His mother had to take a job running a small shop in Goose Gate. His mother spoke encouraging words to her son. "Be good, William, and all will be well."[82] William witnessed the desperation of destitute men and women being **evicted** from their homes. It was common to see children crying and begging on the streets for bread. This impacted him greatly and **forged** the path he took in life.

evicted: forced
forged: directed

William Is Saved

When William was 15, he began attending the Broad Street Wesleyan Chapel, a part of the Methodist Church. The preacher warned his listeners that souls die every minute. William wondered where his soul would go if he were to die. The longer he attended the church, the more William began to recognize the depth of his own sin. While walking home one night after attending a church service, William was convinced that he must repent of his sin. He realized he must make some things right with others. He had deceived a friend who had given him a silver pencil case in return for a favor the friend thought William had done for him. William had kept the pencil case wrongly. He knew he had to humble himself and return it to the friend. "I remember as if but yesterday … the finding of this young fellow I had chiefly wronged, the acknowledgement of my sin, the return of the pencil case—the instant rolling away from my heart of the guilty burden, the peace that came in its place, and the going forth to serve my God and my generation from that hour. 'God shall have all there is of William Booth,' he declared."[83]

William Has an Opportunity to Preach

William had a good friend named Bill Sansom. One day, Bill told William that he and a few friends from the Bible class had decided to start preaching in the poorest sections of the city. He invited William to join the group. William was thankful for the opportunity to share the gospel. Sometimes people ignored them, some said unkind things to them, but some listened. The boys called themselves "The Mission." They continued week after week to preach the gospel. They began to meet in a widow's cottage. One night Bill did not show up. William went to his house and found out that he was very sick with **tuberculosis**. It was not long before Bill died. The other boys in The Mission looked to William for leadership, and he accepted the role.

tuberculosis: a disease of the lungs

William had the opportunity to speak to a man named Besom Jack. He was known for having a terrible temper and often being drunk. As he listened to William preach, he fell to his knees and cried out, "God forgive me for I am a terrible sinner."[84] William knelt next to Besom and led him to the Lord. It was soon evident to all that Besom was a changed man. This led other men in the slums to come listen, and many soon were repenting of their sins.

Off to London

William's apprenticeship ended. He realized he needed to find work to help support his mother and sisters. He decided to move to London to find work as a pawnbroker, although his heart was not in it. What he really cared about was the volunteer work he did after the pawnshop closed. Soon, the Walworth Chapel in London asked William to preach on Sundays. Among those who heard him preach was Edward Rabbit, a prosperous businessman in London. He liked William's preaching and invited William to dinner at his home. There, William met Catherine Mumford. William and Catherine spent much of the evening talking. Catherine was well-read and shared many of the same convictions William held. The more they came to know each other, the more William began to see that they could accomplish more together than they could apart, and he proposed. The couple was married on June 16, 1855.

A month before their wedding, William was appointed to the office of evangelist for a branch of the Methodist denomination in England. Once married, the couple traveled extensively to hold revival meetings. William was fully ordained in 1858 and assigned to Gateshead, a town with a population of 50,000. William and Catherine printed flyers and distributed them from door to door. They organized street meetings and drew curious crowds by singing hymns. They invited the listeners to come to church. In about a year, membership of Bethesda Chapel, the main church in the Gateshead circuit, increased from 39 to 300. The church had a seating capacity of 1,200 but often could not seat all who came to hear William preach. He had a dramatic presentation of the gospel and a powerful, enthusiastic voice that carried well throughout the large building. Catherine visited women in their homes during the week. People gave Bethesda Chapel the nickname of "the converting shop" because so many people were devoting their lives to the Lord.

Preaching Opportunities

The church was not the only thing that was growing. Between 1856 and 1860, Catherine gave birth to the first four of their eight children. Catherine and William taught their children the Word of God from an early age. William was offered a preaching opportunity in the small village of Hayle in Cornwall, England. Each day, more and more people attended special preaching meetings. Fishermen rowed 10 miles through rough seas, and some families hiked over rough coastal paths to hear William. People flocked to the front of the church to confess their sins to the Lord—tough miners, older ladies, and young people. News spread to nearby towns; more than 1,000 people joined local churches. During the 18 weeks William preached in the Cornwall area, 7,000 people professed salvation.

Back to London

Not everyone was happy with William's preaching, however. The Methodist church ordered pastors to stop inviting William to preach. They felt revival meetings were undignified. William and

Catherine had witnessed the positive results that revival meetings produced. They were dedicated to continuing the meetings. They decided to move back to London. Here, their fifth child was born. Instead of holding meetings in churches, William rented a circus tent. Immediately, he noticed that outdoor meetings attracted more sinners, such as **pickpockets** and men with drinking problems. He joyfully told Catherine, "Godless surroundings attract godless people."[85] William saw more opportunities to share the gospel—after all, it was sinners who needed to be saved. He began letting converted sinners share their stories of how God had changed their hearts and behavior. Other sinners listened with **rapt** attention. For the next two years, William preached throughout England and Wales. Two Welsh brothers who had been saved committed to supplying the Booths with living expenses. In the spring of 1864, Catherine gave birth to their sixth child, a daughter.

pickpockets: people who stole from others

rapt: captivated

row houses: a row of houses joined together

deplorable: very bad

London's East End

In July 1865, the East End Revival Society hired William to conduct revival meetings inside an old circus tent. They explained that over one million people lived within a mile of the tent. Nine out of ten had never heard the gospel. The **row houses** in which people lived were run down and dirty. Sometimes 40 or 50 people lived in one house. They had no running water; conditions were **deplorable**. William preached as people began to trickle in. Six people came forward to give their lives to the Lord. William walked eight miles home and burst in to tell Catherine, "I have found my destiny.

I have found a place where there is so much human misery in such a small space that there is a lifetime's work for me. Why go farther afield for audiences when they lie at our doorstep?"[86]

Catherine had never seen him so excited. William would walk the long eight miles every day to conduct evening services. On Sundays, he went in the morning and stayed until after the evening service. Not everyone appreciated William's preaching. Sometimes, he returned home bruised and bloodied. Sometimes, his clothes were torn. Other times, people threw rotten eggs or tomatoes at him, but it did not **deter** him. William felt a deep love for these people, and over time, they began to sense it. Booth shared his mission with others; soon he had a few wealthy men commit to sending him support.

deter: stop

marmoset: South American monkey with a long tail

In November, William moved his family to London's East End so he could spend more time with them. A seventh child was born on Christmas Day. William delighted in spending time with his family. He had a fun-loving nature, and it showed in his play with the children. Their home was filled with pets: guinea pigs, dogs, white mice, birds, and even a **marmoset**. William sang loudly each morning as he dressed and ran up and down the stairs to

amuse the children.

The children all wanted to be a part of their father's life-giving work. Their home was always open to traveling evangelists and preachers. The children loved reenacting the stories of the Bible. His son Ballington pretended to be a preacher like his father. He coaxed his sisters to bring their dolls to attend "services." He later recalled attending a meeting with his father when he was a teenager. Looking upon the misery of the crowd made him feel sick to his stomach. His father told him, "These are our people. These are the people I want you to live for and bring to Christ."[87] Booth called his ministry "The East London Christian Mission."

Ministry Grows

On Christmas Day 1868, William was walking home to watch the children open their gifts. He was struck with the hopelessness of so many people living on the streets hungry and hopeless. He determined that from now on, his family would bake Christmas puddings and distribute them in the slums every Christmas Day. The British Parliament was beginning to take notice of William's work and had started sending some money to help fight poverty. The ministry grew in leaps and bounds. William's eight- and ten-year-old daughters wanted to get involved. They would gather groups of poor children and share the gospel with them. They opened a soup kitchen that served cheap but nutritious meals to more than 2,000 people. William opened reading rooms where people could rest and take refuge from the cold.

The Salvation Army

As time passed, William found other men to help in the ministry. One of them was Elijah Cadman, a young man who had been saved and was eager to join the battle for souls. Elijah drew up posters to notify people of upcoming meetings. He called for 2,000 men and women to join what he named "The Hallelujah Army." He said he was a captain in the Army and called William the general. The idea attracted crowds. Thereafter, William was called General Booth; helpers took on military names. The name of their ministry was changed to The Salvation Army. They were fighting for the souls of men, women, and children. William and his family began training others to go out into the field. The Army grew rapidly, and William started publishing a magazine entitled *The War Cry*. Money raised from the profitable sales was used for operating funds.

Some people wanted to support the Army's efforts but had no

money to contribute. Instead, they began bringing used furniture, clothing, and other items the Army could sell to the public to raise funds. This not only helped the Salvation Army, but it helped reform the slums as well. Poor families were enabled to furnish their meager homes with used merchandise. William purchased big trucks to pick up donations.

William continued to find opportunities to preach the gospel. Once he traveled 800 miles and spoke to 40,000 people in eight days. William and Catherine held meetings from one end of the country to the other. The ministry was beginning to earn respect. Catherine wrote, "It looks like a miracle! Of course it is God who does these things for us. The Lord still shows Himself strong on behalf of those who serve Him with a perfect heart."[88] As news of the work of the Salvation Army spread, many pleas came in from all around the world. William and Catherine realized that the Salvation Army needed to become an international organization. As the Booths' children got older, they began to take leadership roles within the organization.

In November 1881, William raised £15,000 to buy an old building previously used as an orphanage. Here, under the direction of his son Ballington, men were trained to go out and establish new chapters of the Salvation Army. Booth's daughter Evangeline began to work in the ministry when she was 17. She later became the commander of The Salvation Army that began in the United States.

Her work was endorsed by Presidents Theodore Roosevelt, Taft, Wilson, Harding, Coolidge, Hoover, and Franklin D. Roosevelt.

What had started many years ago as a ministry conducted in William and Catherine Booth's home now **encompassed** the entire world. In addition to America, chapters were begun in Australia, France, Canada, Switzerland, the British Isles, Germany, Holland, Denmark, **Zululand**, Norway, Belgium, New Zealand, South Africa, and India. When William died on August 21, 1912, at age 83, there were 16,000 Salvation Army officers serving in 58 countries around the world. The Booths had eight children and 44 grandchildren. All went into full-time Christian work, many in the Salvation Army. The influence of this amazing family is still felt today.

encompassed: included

Zululand: now known as KwaZulu-Natal province in South Africa.

The Salvation Army now exists in 80 countries. New programs have been added to some chapters to include disaster relief, daycare centers, summer camps, hospital and medical facilities, career counseling, vocational training, and homeless shelters. Commissioned officers are still trained to proclaim the gospel and carry on the vision established by William and Catherine Booth. Shortly before he died, William was asked the secret of his success. He unhesitatingly replied, "I will tell you the secret. God has had all there was of me. And if there is anything of power in The Salvation Army today, it is because God has all the adoration of my heart, all the power of my will, and all the influence of my life."[89]

9

Dwight L. Moody

Devoted Evangelist

1837–1899

“*Someday you will read in the papers that D. L. Moody is dead. Don't you believe a word of it! At that moment, I shall be more alive than I am now.*”

Northfield, Massachusetts (USA) – Born in 1837 and moved to Boston as a young man, where he was converted. Passed away there in 1899.

Chicago, Illinois – Founded the Moody Bible Institute and became one of the most well-known evangelists in America.

England – Preached internationally, drawing large crowds.

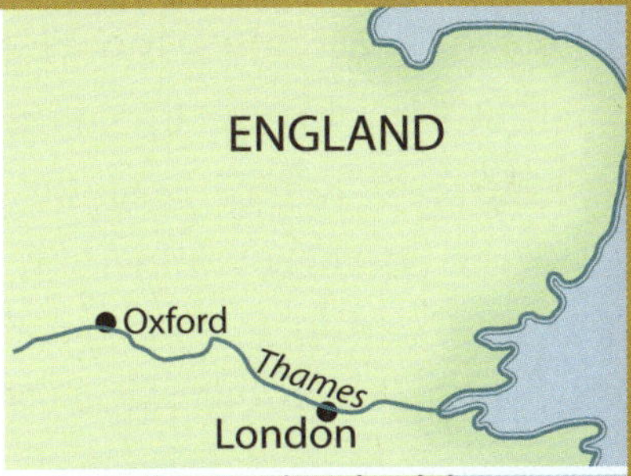

Who Was Dwight Moody?

Known as the greatest evangelist of the 19th century, Dwight L. Moody developed a deep passion for pointing souls to Christ. He grew up in an **impoverished** family and had very little schooling. This contributed to his compassion for people who grew up in the slums. Historians estimate that more than one million people found new life in Jesus Christ in response to his preaching. He established schools for young men and women to equip them to share the gospel. His preaching ministry extended across America and to the British Isles. He helped create the Moody Bible Institute in Chicago, Illinois, which has trained thousands of Christian workers.

impoverished: very poor

distraught: very upset

Early Years

Dwight L. Moody was born on February 5, 1837, on a small family farm in Northfield, Massachusetts. He was the sixth of nine children. When he was only four, Dwight begged his mother to let him attend school with his brothers. He had a bright mind and kept up with the students. He was even able to recite the names of all the presidents in order. Tragically, on an ordinary school day, a neighbor entered the classroom and announced that the Moody children's father had suddenly died. They hurried home to find their mother **distraught**. To add to her distress, she was expecting twins to be born the following month.

Dwight's father had accumulated a lot of debt. Soon, debt collectors started to come around. Friends and relatives tried to persuade Betsy, Dwight's mother, to give the children away to families with the means to provide for them. However, Betsy was determined to keep her family together. Dwight was grateful that his mother made that decision. Betsy's two brothers offered to pay the **mortgage** so the family could keep the house. Betsy brought her children to church every Sunday. She regularly read to them from the Bible, the only book the family owned. Each child had one pair of shoes. They would walk to church barefoot and put their shoes on just before entering the building to keep the shoes from wearing out too quickly.

mortgage: payment

Dwight's older brothers had to earn money to support the family. When Dwight was ten, it was his turn to go to work in nearby Greenfield. His schooling ended, and Dwight went to work for an elderly couple, milking their cow and doing farm chores. He met a man in Greenfield who noticed he was new to the town. The man observed that Dwight looked lonely, so he told the young boy that he had a friend who sticks more closely than a brother. That friend was Jesus Christ. He gave Dwight a shiny penny. Dwight had never had any money of his own! After two months, he went home to help his mother on the farm, but he always remembered that nice man, the first person who told him about having a personal relationship with Jesus Christ.

A Shoe Salesman

A week after Dwight's seventeenth birthday, he decided to make his own way in the world. He headed off for Boston and went to see his Uncle Samuel, the owner of a successful shoe store. He asked for a job. Jobs were scarce in Boston. His uncle had hesitations about Dwight and told him so. He knew Dwight liked to run things and was **headstrong** and full of opinions. He reluctantly gave Dwight a job but required some **stipulations**. Uncle Samuel's first requirement was that Dwight follow orders and not tell the other employees how to do their jobs. Then, he must stay at a **reputable** boarding house. Third, he was not to go out partying at night. Finally, he had to agree to attend Mount Vernon Church every Sunday for both Sunday school and church. Dwight happily accepted. "I'll do it all, Uncle. You don't have to worry about me. I'll be the best employee you ever had, and I won't boss the others around, although I do have a few ideas about the window display."[90]

headstrong: stubborn

stipulations: conditions he must agree to

reputable: well-thought-of

Mr. Kimball

Mount Vernon Church was a Congregational church. It was quite different from the Unitarian church Dwight had attended in Northfield. The Unitarian church did not believe that Jesus was the Son of God but rather a good man who had lived on earth. His Sunday school teacher, Mr. Kimball, spoke about a new life in Jesus Christ, encouraging the students to read from the Gospel of John. Dwight felt ignorant.

Dwight began to attend the YMCA, an organization for young men founded to provide instruction in the Bible and to encourage prayer. It was a safe place for young men to gather and do physical exercise. It also had a reading room and a free library. It operated in the Old South Church in Boston. Dwight continued attending church and listened as the pastor preached about accepting Christ as Savior. Dwight did not understand this but felt sure he could wait until he was older to deal with it.

That was the case until one Saturday morning, April 21, 1855. He was working in the shoe store as usual when Mr. Kimball, his Sunday school teacher, entered the store. Tearfully, he approached Dwight and said, "Dwight, God loves you. His son Jesus Christ died for you. Dwight, I want to know if you believe that."[91] Dwight said no one had ever asked him that before. Yes, he did believe that.

He believed that Jesus Christ died for his sins, and he wanted to begin to live like it was true. Dwight felt like a new man. He felt a consuming desire to read his Bible and pray.

Moving to Chicago

Nineteen-year-old Dwight loved selling shoes and was quite successful, but he was not very good at following orders. He soon had a dispute with his uncle. Dwight decided to move to Chicago and find a job there as a shoe salesman. He obtained a position in Wiswall's Shoe Store. Seeing Dwight's enthusiasm and energy, the owner sent him to the train station to meet **immigrants** as they **disembarked** to sell boots to the newcomers.

> **immigrants:** persons who come to live permanently in a foreign country
>
> **disembarked:** stepped off the train

Dwight was very successful. He determined to become a millionaire and began investing money in land, selling it at a profit. He wrote to his brother George, "I tell you hear (this is how Dwight spelled the word "here." Remember, he did not attend school for very long) is the place to make money, and that is not all. I have enjoyed more Religion hear than I have ever in my life. I find the better I live, the more enjoyment I have."[92]

In his spare time, Dwight wanted to be involved in Christian work. Someone told him to go to Wells Street Mission to see if he could be of help there. He felt he could not teach because of his poor grammar. The man in charge suggested he recruit disadvantaged boys to attend. Dwight was extremely successful in this endeavor. At his first attempt, he brought in 18 barefooted boys. He threw himself wholeheartedly into what he called "drumming up scholars." Every Sunday Dwight brought in more new children. After two years, Wells Street Sunday School was outgrowing its space. Dwight decided to start a new mission Sunday school in another location in Chicago.

North Market Hall

In the fall of 1858, he found North Market Hall, a huge, **dilapidated** brick building, and committed to renting it for a year. He learned that on Saturday nights it was rented out to a German group that held a large dance. They never cleaned up afterward, so Dwight did that task each Sunday morning. After cleaning, scrubbing, and setting up hundreds of chairs, he set out to recruit children. Dwight was armed with plenty of rock candy to help coax the children to come. He would say, "No Sunday

dilapidated: in need of repair

school, no sweets."[93] Sometimes he helped children get washed up and offered to wait while they ran to get their brothers and sisters. Frequently, he rode the streets on a pony, which not only attracted the children but helped him cover more ground. The children loved taking turns riding the pony. The children considered him a wonderful friend.

Sunday school began at 2 p.m. Dwight would lead the large procession of rowdy street children back to the hall for Sunday school. Often there were 1,000 children present. After Sunday school, Dwight set out again visiting the neighborhoods to invite folks to the evening service. After the evening service, he spent time praying with people who had special needs. He did this week after week.

Some of the parents started attending lessons and evening services as well. Volunteers offered to teach and staff the Sunday school. Dwight considered his job to be rounding up the children. He preferred that others would do the teaching. As time passed, he filled in for absent teachers and found that he enjoyed telling Bible stories. The children always loved it when he spoke to them. The parents asked him to speak at family meetings, and he soon enjoyed doing this too.

Full-time Service

By 1858, Dwight ran the largest Sunday school in the United States. He also spent hours selling shoes during the week. Dwight knew the importance of having a personal relationship with Christ. He became deeply concerned that he needed to communicate this clearly to both children and parents. Although making a lot of money had been a personal goal since he had entered the shoe sales business, he was coming to see that he could reach more people if he were to give up his business goals and commit his life to bringing people to salvation in Christ. He told a friend, "What I must decide is whether or not now is the right time to abandon my job as a salesman and devote myself fully to God's work."[94]

One contributing factor was that he had met and proposed to Emma Revell, who had been helping in the ministry. Dwight told Emma his plan to quit his job and she replied, "I will stand with you, whatever you decide to do, D.L., and I am confident God will help us face the future together."[95] In November 1860, newly elected President Abraham Lincoln visited Chicago and having heard of Moody's Sunday school, decided to attend. Dwight asked him to say a few words to the children. Lincoln

was impressed by the ministry and encouraged the children, saying, "Govern your lives according to the precepts you learn from your study of the Bible."[96]

Civil War

The coming of the Civil War offered Dwight more opportunities to share the gospel. Chicago was a major hub, as it was located between major rivers and railroads. Recruits were housed in makeshift tents at what was called Camp Douglas. Dwight called for volunteers to preach to the soldiers, and 150 men responded. By November, Camp Douglas was base to 4,200 Union soldiers, and Dwight was asked to take leadership of the "Christian Commission." Its goal was to minister to the soldiers and urge them to repent, realizing they might be killed in battle. Many of the 12,000 Confederate soldiers who had been captured were transferred to Camp Douglas. Dwight was granted permission to hold services for the Confederate prisoners of war as well.

Dwight and Emma were married on August 28, 1862, in a quiet family ceremony. They moved into a small house on the north side of Chicago, near North Market Hall. A little girl, named Emma after her mother, was born to the couple in October 1864. Dwight was having trouble getting new converts to attend established churches. Some church members did not want to receive the usually ragged street people. Often the street people could not understand the flowery sermons expounded in established churches.

Dwight decided to start a street church where all people—young, old, rich, or poor—would be welcome. On December 30, the Illinois Street Church was dedicated. It was a nondenominational, independent church. Moody made it clear that it was not his church; the church belonged to all who attended. He invited students from Chicago Theological Seminary to preach each Sunday. One Sunday, a student who was supposed to preach failed to show up and Dwight was forced to fill in. People responded well and wanted him to continue preaching.

Visit to England

Emma began struggling with **asthma**. Her doctor recommended she visit the seashore. The couple left little Emma with Emma's mother and headed for England. Dwight was excited at the thought of meeting Charles Spurgeon and George Müller. They visited the Metropolitan Tabernacle on their first Sunday in England and heard the famous Charles Spurgeon preach. It was a dream come true for Dwight.

asthma: an inflammatory lung

pondered: gave serious and careful thought

Dwight was given many opportunities to preach while in England, and he was fortunate to sit under other pastors. In one sermon that affected him greatly, the preacher said, "The world has yet to see what God can do with and for and through and in and by the man who is fully and wholly consecrated to Him."[97] Dwight **pondered** the fact that the preacher did not say the man had to be well-schooled or eloquent in speech, just consecrated. He determined from that day forward he would be that man, serving God with all that he had.

Ira Sankey

Dwight and Emma sailed back to America. They were glad to be home again. One night during a church service, a deep baritone voice sang out from the back of the church. When the service was over, Dwight went to find the man with the rich-sounding voice. His name was Ira

Sankey. Dwight persuaded him to move his family to Chicago to accompany him in ministry. Moody would preach and Sankey would sing. Crowds were attracted to both the singing and the preaching, and the Illinois Street Church continued to grow.

Disaster struck the city on October 8, 1871, when the great Chicago fire destroyed much of the town, including Moody's home and the church. Three hundred people lost their lives in that disastrous fire; 100,000 were left homeless, and property damage totaled over $222 million. Dwight wrote letters to friends in the Sunday School Union, the Christian Commission, and the YMCA to raise funds to rebuild the church. On December 24, 1871, the new North Side Tabernacle was dedicated. The church overflowed with attendees and soon Sunday school resumed. Doors were left unlocked so people who were homeless could find shelter when they needed it. Chicago began to be rebuilt.

Preaching Overseas

Dwight and Ira conducted many services overseas in England, Scotland, and Ireland. Churches were filled to the brim and as one man put it, "The church was crowded in every part and every spot of standing ground occupied. A number have come to peace in believing—some of them most unlikely."[98] Dwight Moody and his song leader, Ira Sankey, became famous throughout Europe. Moody preached to a crowd of approximately 30,000 from the box of a carriage in the Botanical Gardens during the closing of one of their campaigns in Scotland. Revival broke out in Scotland. One Scotsman observed that "The whole religious tone of Scotland has been lifted up and brightened most remarkably."[99]

Dwight and Ira conducted services throughout the British Isles. In England alone, Moody preached to over 2.5 million people. Eight years after he and Emma had listened to Charles Spurgeon preach, Dwight stood preaching to Spurgeon and his congregation from that very pulpit. He had intended to spend six months in the British Isles but instead stayed more than two years. He made seven trips to the British Isles in his lifetime, spreading the good news of Jesus Christ.

Moody Bible Institute

Dwight dreamed of opening a school for girls in Northfield, his old hometown in Massachusetts. It became known as Wellesley College; it still exists today. He raised the money to build the school. Its main goal was to make the Bible the primary curriculum. Then, each girl would be involved in the domestic duties required to run the school; thirdly, the cost of tuition would be kept at half the cost of educating each girl. The school would cover the other half. At the school's dedication, Dwight spoke, "My lack of education had always been a disadvantage to me … I hope after all of us who are here today are dead and gone, this school may live and be a blessing to the world and that missionaries may go out from here and preach the gospel to the **heathen**, and it may be recognized as a power in bringing souls to Christ."[100] Soon a school was established in Northfield for boys as well.

heathen: one who does not believe in religion

mechanical reaping machine: a horse-drawn machine that revolutionized agriculture

In May 1889, Dwight was back in Chicago. He saw a need for a Bible institute in the city and began raising support. He was given $5,000 to build such a school. Cyrus McCormick, inventor of the **mechanical reaping machine**, contributed $100,000 to the school. Money poured in from many sources. Dormitories were built for both young men and young women. That year, students conducted over 3,000 meetings and made 10,000 visits to the homes of the poor. Graduates went as missionaries to India, China, Africa, South America, Turkey, Bulgaria, Persia, Burma, and Japan. At the end of 10 years, more than 3,000 students had enrolled, tuition-free, in buildings then worth one-third of a million dollars. One-third of the graduates had gone into full-time Christian service. The rest filled lay positions in churches that stretched across the country. This school became the well-known Moody Bible Institute that still functions today.

On to Heaven

Dwight's heart was beginning to suffer. His doctor told him he must slow down, but slowing down was not something Dwight knew how to do. In November 1899, he set out on a campaign to Kansas City, Missouri. As Moody stepped from the train in Kansas City, he felt the old throbbing in his chest. Despite that, he insisted on preaching but finally had to admit he needed to head home without completing the full schedule. He made it to Northfield, but his health continued to decline. On December 22, 1899, he told his son that God was calling him. He praised his dear wife and then passed from earth to heaven. He had often preached, "Someday you will read in the papers that D. L. Moody is dead. Don't you believe a word of it! At that moment, I shall be more alive than I am now. … I was born of the flesh in 1837. I was born of the Spirit in 1856. That which is born of the flesh may die. That which is born of the Spirit will live forever."[101]

10

John Harper

Hero of the Titanic

1872–1912

"Believe in the Lord Jesus Christ and you will be saved."

Houston, Scotland – Born in 1872 and felt called to ministry at an early age.

Glasgow, Scotland – Became a Baptist pastor and was widely known for his passionate preaching.

London, England – Pastored Walworth Road Baptist Church before setting sail for America.

North Atlantic Ocean – Died in 1912 during the sinking of the *Titanic*, reportedly preaching to others in the water until his last breath.

Who Was John Harper?

John Harper was a Scottish Baptist pastor with a successful ministry. He began preaching on street corners to all who would listen. He became the pastor of Paisley Road Baptist Church in Glasgow, Scotland, in 1897. Harper's reputation as a dynamic evangelist was well-known. In 1912, he was invited for a second time to speak for several weeks at the Moody Bible Church in Chicago. He took passage on the maiden voyage of the *Titanic* and died when the ship sank in the North Atlantic Ocean.

Early Years

John Harper was born on May 29, 1872, in the village of Houston, Scotland. He and his older brother George grew up in a Christian home. George recalled an incident that happened when John was only two years old. The boys were playing a game near the deep spring well at the edge of the family garden. John stumbled, falling into the well. George remembered crying out to his mother, who came and rescued little John. She turned him upside down and held

him by his feet to expel the water from his lungs. John had nearly drowned, but God had preserved his life. Both John and his brother attended the Board School in their village. This was the only formal schooling John ever received. The family was impoverished, so the boys had to earn income to help support the family.

John Is Converted

George and John were both saved within three months of each other. It was on a Sunday night in March 1886 that John, age 13, surrendered his life to the Savior. He attended church at the village free pulpit. Two preachers spoke that night: Dr. Walter B. Sloan and Mr. Archibald Ewing. The preachers expounded on John 3:16. At the end of the service an invitation was extended for any person to stay behind who wanted more information. John was "led to see God's rich provision in Jesus for his salvation."[102] Their parents had taught their sons the Scriptures from the time they were young boys. They learned to pray and reverence the Word of God. That night, however, God extended his salvation to young John Harper who, for the remainder of his life, had a burning zeal to live for his Lord. His father was thrilled that his prayers for his son's salvation had been answered.

As a young man, John worked in a mill. When he was 18 years old, he felt a strong compulsion to spend his life preaching the gospel to a dying world. He began to spend all his free time preaching in his village. He would plead with anyone who would listen to give their lives to the Lord. John could "never tell of having wandered far from God, and far into sin. Yet under God he was the means of leading numbers to the Savior who had gone far astray."[103]

John was an eager student of the Bible. He read any commentaries he could get his hands on and memorized and meditated on the Word. He had a gift for explaining the Word to others using a unique way of quoting Scripture that people seemed to remember. Once, quoting 1 John 1:7, he repeated the words "all sin" three times over for emphasis: "The blood of Jesus Christ, God's Son, cleanseth us from all sin, ALL SIN, ALL SIN."

Full-time Christian Service

After John had been preaching every evening after work for six years, he was asked to work in a Baptist Mission in Govan in Glasgow, Scotland. There, John was set apart for the gospel ministry. Though still very young, John was **fervent** in his preaching. A man from the city heard him preaching one night and inquired, "Who is that man who is preaching for all he is worth?"[104] After one and a half years of ministering in Govan, John was invited to pastor a newly formed church called the Paisley Road Baptist Church in Gordon Halls. Years later, after John's death, the name of the church was changed to Harper Memorial Church.

fervent: passionate

Church members of all ages began helping John preach on street corners, outside public buildings, or anywhere they could draw listeners. John's zeal and enthusiasm for souls was contagious. It was transmitted to his helpers, and many came to know Christ as Savior. The church began with 25 members, but under John's leadership, it grew to over 500

members. After four years, they outgrew the Gordon Hall's facility and moved to Plantation Street. There, they constructed a large iron building that could hold 500 to 600 people. An 80-year-old church member was asked to relate how he had come to trust Christ. He explained that he had just turned 70 when, "I was just passing Plantation, and **yon** man, Mr. Harper, was preaching at the street corner, and I trusted the Lord there and then."[105]

yon: a person over there

Family Life

On April 28, 1903, John Harper married Anne Leckie Bell. They lived in Denmark Hill, Surrey, England. A little daughter, Annie Jessie (nicknamed Nana), was born to the couple on January 1, 1906. Sadly, Anne died on January 8 due to complications from childbirth. John's cousin Jessie Leitch helped him care for little Nana.

Two More Close Calls

George also recalled how John, at age 26, had another near-drowning experience. George and John were working together in mission work. They were known as "The Harper Brothers." One beautiful day, while enjoying the seaside, they decided to take a dip in the water. Neither young man could swim. The tide was strong and receding. Caught in the undertow, they were soon in danger of drowning. They furiously fought the tide and, though exhausted, were miraculously saved from disaster. The brothers bowed their knees and thanked God for preserving their lives.

Again, when John was 32 years old, he was on a trip with a friend. They were aboard a ship on the Mediterranean Sea when suddenly the ship sprang a leak. They were providentially rescued after many hours of wondering whether they would be found in time. John described his experience this way: "The fear of death did not for one moment disturb me. I believed that sudden death would be sudden glory, but there was a wee motherless girl in Glasgow, and, oh, I thought, if I had only committed her to my dear brother George's care before I left."[106]

John Harper Is Invited to Speak at Moody Church

After serving as pastor for 13 years, John was called to London to pastor the Walworth Road Church. The church grew rapidly in the two years he pastored there. In 1912, an invitation arrived for John to conduct three months of special services at the Moody

Church in Chicago, where he had preached about two years before. The meetings in 1910 had been such a success that more people came to hear John than had come to the church since the passing of D.L. Moody 12 years earlier. The church had, therefore, invited him to return. John was scheduled to sail for America on the ship *Lusitania*, but at the last moment, the schedule changed, and John decided to leave earlier on the *Titanic*. A dear friend was alarmed at his announcement. He told John he dreamed that disaster awaited John if he went ahead with plans to leave on the *Titanic*. The dream did not deter John, however. There were souls to be preached to in America, and he was determined to do it.

maiden: first-ever

The *Titanic*

John's six-year-old daughter Nana and his niece Jessie accompanied him on his journey to Chicago. The *Titanic* had been built for the White Star Line. She would be taking her **maiden** voyage. It was the largest vessel ever made, over four city blocks in length. She had a crew of 860 and could hold up to 2500 passengers. "Not only was the *Titanic* the largest steamship afloat but it was the most luxurious. Elaborately furnished cabins opened onto her eleven decks."[107] The ship "was equipped with a gymnasium, swimming pool, hospital with an operating room, and a grill and palm garden."[108] It contained a huge refrigerator with separate rooms to store beef, poultry, fruit, fish, vegetables, butter, bacon, and cheese, among other foods. Each room in the refrigerator was maintained with temperatures suitable for the type of food it stored. The ship was a marvel of shipbuilding. She had an elaborate system of watertight compartments that supposedly made her unsinkable.

An employee of the White Star Line boasted, "Not even God himself could sink this ship."[109]

The ship set sail on April 10, 1912, from Southampton, England. It was bound for New York City. Crowds of onlookers assembled to wave goodbye to the passengers, many of them famous people. Notable passengers on board included Major Butt, a military aide to President Taft; John Jacob Astor, one of the world's wealthiest men and his new bride; and Benjamin Guggenheimer, who had made his fortune in his **smelting** and refining company. Also on board were Isidor Straus and his wife, co-owners of Macy's Department Stores. They were known for generously giving to charitable organizations. Among the passengers were famous financiers, steel manufacturers, journalists, shipbuilders, and many others. Mr. Bruce Ismay was aboard. He was part-owner of the ship *Titanic* and managing director of the White Star Line.

smelting: the extraction of metal from its ore by a process of heating and melting it

The voyage went smoothly at first. On Sunday, April 14, John Harper, his niece, and his daughter had morning prayers and attended the morning church service aboard the ship. That evening, Jessie and Nana found John engaged in a conversation with a young Englishman, urging him to place his faith in Jesus Christ. Jessie recalled that, before heading off to bed with Nana, they all stood on the deck enjoying the colorful sunset. John commented, "It will be beautiful in the morning."[110]

The *Titanic* Strikes an Iceberg

Earlier, on Sunday afternoon, the *Titanic's* wireless operator received a message stating, "The German steamship *Amerika* (Hamburg-American Line) reports by radio telegraph passing two large icebergs in latitude 41.27, longitude 50.08."[111] Thomas Whitely, a steward on the ship, related later that he heard two of the lookouts on the crow's nest issue a warning. "I heard one of them say that at 11:15 o'clock, 15 minutes before the *Titanic* struck, he had reported to the First Officer Murdock, on the bridge, that he fancied he saw an iceberg! Twice after that, the lookout said, he warned Murdock that an iceberg was ahead. They were quite **indignant** that no attention was paid to their warnings."[112]

indignant: upset
heralded: advertised

At 11:40 p.m., the massive ship, **heralded** as unsinkable, struck a giant iceberg. The side of the ship was ripped open, letting water flow freely through the once watertight compartments. The *Titanic* was at 41.46 latitude, 50.14 longitude, near Newfoundland, Canada. Many passengers never felt the impact. Many were sleeping. Others were in restaurants or playing games.

The *Titanic* Sinks

The captain immediately instructed the crew to shut the emergency doors but was told they had already been shut. Seawater was flooding the ship. It was rapidly **listing** forward. The engines were put to work pumping out water, but it was filling up too fast. Distress signals were sent out and all the crew were ordered to appear on the deck. Stewards were told to wake up sleeping passengers. The cry was heard, "All passengers on deck with life belts!"[113]

listing: leaning

Panic struck as passengers came to the awful realization that their lives were in danger. The officers began to cut loose the lifeboats. The order was given for all the men to stand to one side. Women were told to go to B deck with their children. The officers manning the lifeboats directed the women to the front and the men to the rear. Men were commanded to "Stand back! The women come first."[114]

The captain ordered the band to play to help settle the passengers. They played, among other hymns, "Nearer my God to Thee." Many men heroically helped to see that women and children were safely placed in lifeboats and lowered into the dark sea. Tragically, there were not enough lifeboats to save all the passengers. There were 2,340 passengers with only 20 lifeboats. Each lifeboat could fit 50 passengers and eight crew members to man it. Four lifeboats were destroyed while cutting them loose. Some of the boats drifted away before they were filled to capacity. Only 711 people were safely launched in lifeboats. The rest were left to jump into the icy waters, hoping to be rescued. Six people in the lifeboats died from exposure. The night was frightfully cold. The temperature of the Atlantic Ocean was 28 degrees F (-2 C). Some passengers were in their night clothes; no one was dressed warmly enough for such frigid temperatures. The total number of passengers saved was 705. Sadly, 1,635 people lost their lives that night. The captain, E.J. Smith, an admiral of the White Star Fleet, went down with his ship.

John Harper — *Titanic's* Last Hero

John Harper, when made aware of the great danger, had hurried to lift Jessie and Nana onto the eleventh lifeboat, praying for their safety. He then rushed back to help the frightened people who were still on the ship. Two hours and forty minutes after the ship struck the iceberg, the big stern of the ship rose in the air and the ship went down bow first. John was among the 1528 passengers who were either thrown into the icy waters or forced to jump. For over an hour, John swam determinedly from one person to another. People were quickly succumbing to **hypothermia** in the freezing water. John was bringing the dying people the message of hope in the gospel of Jesus Christ. Only half a dozen people survived who were floating in the icy waters without a lifeboat that night. Survivors testified to seeing

hypothermia: when the body loses heat faster than it can produce it, often leading to death.

John preaching the gospel to the end. It was two hours before the British passenger liner, *Carpathia*, responding to the call of distress dispatched from the sinking ship, was able to reach the survivors.

In 1916, at a meeting of *Titanic* survivors that met in Canada, a young Scotsman named Aquila Webb told the story of what happened that night. He said he was floating on a **spar** in the icy waters after the *Titanic* went down. He floated near John Harper, who was holding onto a piece of wood from the wreck. Harper pleaded with Webb to "Believe in the Lord Jesus Christ, and you will be saved" (Acts 16:31, NASB 1995). Harper then asked Webb if he was saved. Webb told John he was not, and the turbulent sea caused the two to drift apart. Several minutes later, the swirling sea again brought John floating near Webb. John urged Webb to trust Christ for salvation. He asked, "Are you saved yet?" Once again Webb answered, "No." Webb watched as John removed his life jacket, giving it to another man, telling him he needed it more than John did. John was heard to cry out, "I am going down. I am going down. No, no, I am going up."[115] Aquila then watched as John slipped beneath the waves to a watery grave. Aquila Webb, all alone on the dark sea with two miles of icy water under him, attested to the fact that he then bowed his head and placed his trust in the Lord Jesus Christ. He was the last convert of John Harper—hero of the *Titanic*.

spar: strong pole such as the mast of a ship

Note of interest: John Harper's daughter and his niece arrived safely in New York to learn that John had died. The Moody Church sent them money and clothes so they could return to Scotland. Jessie raised Annie who grew up to marry a pastor, had children and grandchildren, and died in 1986.

Timeline

1703 – 1727	1703	John Wesley is born.
	1703	Jonathan Edwards is born.
	1706	Benjamin Franklin is born.
	1714	George Whitefield is born.
	1714	John Wesley goes to Charterhouse School.
	1716	Jonathan Edwards enters Yale.
	1720	John Wesley enters Christ Church, Oxford.
	1722–1723	Jonathan Edwards preaches in New York City.
	1724–1726	Jonathan Edwards tutors at Yale.
	1726	George Whitefield attends St. Mary de Crypt grammar school.
	1727	Jonathan Edwards is ordained at Northampton Presbyterian Church.

1727 – 1737

1727	Jonathan Edwards marries Sarah Pierpont.
1728	John Wesley is ordained.
1729	John Wesley forms the Holy Club.
1732	George Whitefield enters Pembroke College at Oxford University.
1732	The Holy Club is called Methodists.
1733	George Whitefield is invited to join the Holy Club; his health declines from self-denial.
1733	Revival begins in Northampton.
1735	George Whitefield finds salvation in Jesus Christ.
1736	George Whitefield is ordained, begins to preach, and asked to go to Georgia.
1736	John and Charles Wesley go to Georgia in America.
1737	George Whitefield preaches to thousands in Bristol and London.

1738–1742

1738	George Whitefield's first trip to America.
1738	George Whitefield returns to England to raise money for orphanages in Georgia.
1738	John Wesley becomes a Christian.
1739	George Whitefield's second trip to America—becomes an itinerate preacher.
1739–1740	The Great Awakening
1739	John Wesley founds the Methodist Church.
1740	George Whitefield opens Bethesda orphanage in Georgia, preaches to great crowds in America.
1741	Jonathan Edwards preaches "Sinners in the Hand of an Angry God."
1742	George Whitefield preaches in Scotland.
1742	Susanna Wesley dies.

1744–1752

1744	George Whitefield returns to America, gets very sick, recovers and preaches to thousands.
1745	Francis Asbury is born.
1747	David Brainerd visits Jonathan Edwards at Northampton.
1747	John and Charles Wesley begin ministering in Ireland.
1748	George Whitefield becomes chaplain to Lady Huntingdon.
1748	Jonathan Edwards splits from Northampton congregation.
1749	Jonathan Edwards publishes his memorial of David Brainerd.
1751	John Wesley marries Molly Vazeille.
1751–1752	George Whitefield's fourth trip to America.

1752–1765

1752–1754	George Whitefield preaches in Wales, Scotland, and London.
1754–1755	George Whitefield's fifth trip to America.
1755–1763	George Whitefield preaches throughout Great Britain.
1758	Jonathan Edwards is offered the presidency of Princeton University.
1758	Jonathan Edwards takes smallpox vaccine.
1758	Jonathan Edwards dies of smallpox.
1758	Francis Asbury is apprenticed to a buckle maker.
1758	Francis Asbury is converted and commits to dedicate his life to Christian work.
1763–1765	George Whitefield's sixth trip to America; often sick but preaches and is warmly welcomed.

1765–1783		
	1765–1769	George Whitefield preaches in England and London.
	1765	Francis Asbury's apprenticeship is completed, and he decides to become a traveling Methodist preacher.
	1766	Francis Asbury begins his first Methodist circuit.
	1769–1770	George Whitefield's seventh and final trip to America. Preaches his last sermon.
	1770	George Whitefield dies.
	1771	Francis Asbury attends his first Methodist conference.
	1771	Francis Asbury leaves for America.
	1781	Molly Wesley dies.
	1783	Francis Asbury goes to Philadelphia to minister to those with yellow fever.

1784–1802

1784	John Wesley ordains Dr. Thomas Coke to oversee Methodist work in America.
1785	Peter Cartwright is born in Amherst County, Virginia.
1791	John Wesley dies.
1793	Cartwright family moves to Rogue's Harbor, Kentucky.
1799	George Washington dies.
1800	Francis Asbury travels on the Wilderness Road to minister in the west.
1801	Peter Cartwright is saved and baptized.
1801	Peter Cartwright becomes a member of the Methodist Episcopal Church.
1802	Peter Cartwright is given a permit to preach.
1802	Cartwrights move to Lewiston County, Kentucky.
1802	Peter Cartwright attends Brown's Academy.

1803 –1815

1803	Peter Cartwright begins circuit riding.
1804	Lewis and Clark Expedition begins.
1805	George Müller is born.
1806	Peter Cartwright is ordained by Francis Asbury.
1806	Lewis and Clark return from their expedition.
1808	Peter Cartwright marries Frances Gaines.
1810	Eliza is born to Peter and Francis Cartwright.
1812	Maria is born to Peter and Francis Cartwright.
1812	War of 1812 breaks out.
1814	Peter Cartwright joins General Andrew Jackson's army as chaplain.
1815	War of 1812 ends.
1815	George Müller attends the Cathedral School.

1816–1834

1816	Francis Asbury dies.
1824	Peter Cartwright moves to Illinois.
1825	George Müller is saved.
1828	Peter Cartwright is persuaded to run for the legislature, still preaching.
1828	Peter Cartwright helps to found McKendree College.
1829	George Müller goes to England to join London Missionary Society.
1829	William Booth is born.
1830	Knox returns to Geneva with his wife. George Müller becomes pastor at Teignmouth
1830	George Müller marries Mary Groves.
1832	George Müller goes to Bristol.
1832	Lydia Müller is born.
1834	George Müller starts the Scriptural Knowledge Institute.

1834 – 1850

1834	Charles Spurgeon is born.
1836	George Müller opens his first two orphanages.
1837	George Müller opens third orphanage for boys.
1837	D.L. Moody is born.
1841	D.L. Moody's father dies.
1842	William Booth is apprenticed to a buckle maker.
1844	William Booth begins attending the Broad St. Wesleyan Chapel.
1844	William Booth becomes a Christian.
1847	Dwight Moody goes to work to support the family at age 10.
1849	George Müller opens an orphanage at Ashley Downs.
1849	William Booth's apprenticeship ends, and he leaves for London to look for work.
1850	Charles Spurgeon is converted.

1851 –1855		
	1851	Charles Spurgeon preaches his first sermon.
	1852	Charles Spurgeon becomes pastor of Baptist Church at Waterbeach.
	1852	William Booth preaches at Walworth Road Chapel.
	1852	William Booth gives up his job to go into full-time ministry.
	1852	William Booth meets Catherine Mumford and they plan to marry.
	1852	William Booth is offered a job preaching by the Reformed Methodists.
	1854	Charles Spurgeon becomes pastor of New Park Street Church.
	1854	Dwight Moody moves to Boston and gets a job in Uncle Samuel's shoe store.
	1855	Dwight Moody is led to the Lord by his Sunday school teacher.

1855 – 1861		
	1855	William Booth and Catherine are married.
	1856	William Booth's first child is born.
	1856	Charles Spurgeon marries Susanna Thompson.
	1856	Dwight Moody moves to Chicago to sell shoes.
	1857	George Müller opens second orphanage at Ashley Downs.
	1857	The Pastors' College opens — renamed Spurgeon's College in 1923.
	1858	Dwight Moody starts the North Market Hall Sunday school.
	1860	Abraham Lincoln visits North Market Hall Sunday school.
	1860	William Booth's fourth child is born.
	1861	Charles Spurgeon congregation moves to the Metropolitan Tabernacle.
	1861	Civil War begins.

1862 – 1868

1862	George Müller opens third orphanage at Ashley Downs.
1862	Dwight Moody marries Emma Revell in Chicago.
1862	Dwight Moody ministers to soldiers at Camp Douglas.
1863	Emancipation Proclamation is signed by Abraham Lincoln.
1863	William and Catherine Booth go to Wales to minister.
1865	Civil War ends.
1867	Dwight Moody goes to England for the first time.
1867	Charles Spurgeon opens an orphanage for boys.
1868	George Müller opens fourth orphanage at Ashley Downs.
1868	William Booth's eighth child is born.
1868	William Booth decides to take Christmas pudding to all the poor families.

1870 – 1875

1870	George Müller opens fifth orphanage at Ashley Downs.
1870	Mary Müller dies.
1870	Dwight Moody teams up with Ira Sankey.
1871	George Müller marries Susannah Grace.
1871	The Great Chicago fire destroys much of the city.
1872	Peter Cartwright dies.
1872	John Harper is born.
1873	Dwight Moody and Ira Sankey begin two-year campaign in the British Isles.
1874	John Harper falls in a well and almost drowns.
1875	Susanna Spurgeon starts Book Fund to provide Christian books to pastors.
1875	Dwight Moody begins holding large meetings in major American cities.

1876 – 1887

1876	Dwight Moody buys property in Northfield, MA, for a home for girls and one for boys.
1878	The Salvation Army is birthed.
1879	Charles Spurgeon opens an orphanage for girls.
1879	Northfield seminary for young women is established.
1880	William Booth sends representatives to start Salvation Army in America.
1881	Dwight Moody opens Mt. Hermon school for boys.
1881	Dwight Moody goes to United Kingdom again.
1886	William Booth goes to America.
1886	John Harper is saved.
1887	The Salvation Army helps provide shelter and soup kitchens for homeless.

1889–1898		
	1889	Chicago Bible Institute is established (later becomes Moody Bible Institute).
	1889	William Booth decides to write a book.
	1890	Catherine Booth dies.
	1890	John Harper begins to preach.
	1891	Charles Spurgeon preaches his last sermon at Metropolitan Tabernacle.
	1891	William Booth again visits America.
	1892	Charles Spurgeon dies.
	1895	Susannah Müller dies.
	1895	William Booth travels to India and Japan.
	1897	Paisley Road Church, later named Harper Memorial Church, is formed.
	1898	George Müller dies.

1898 – 1908

1898	John Harper is saved from drowning while swimming with his brother.
1899	Dwight Moody holds last meetings in Kansas City, Missouri.
1899	Dwight Moody dies at home at age 62.
1904	John Harper is saved from drowning on a ship that sprang a leak.
1905	William Booth visits Salvation Army in Australia and New Zealand.
1906	John and Annie Harper's little girl is born.
1906	John Harper's wife dies.
1907	William Booth travels again to America.
1908	William Booth travels to Sweden.

1912	1912	William Booth preaches his last sermon in London to 7000 Salvation Army officers.
	1912	William Booth dies.
	1912	John Harper leaves on the *Titanic* to preach at Moody Bible Institute.
	1912	John Harper helps his niece Jessie and his daughter Nana into a lifeboat to escape the sinking *Titanic*.
	1912	John Harper leads his last convert to Christ.
	1912	John Harper dies in icy waters after the *Titanic* sinks.

Glossary

admonition: Teaching and instruction

amplify: Increase the volume

apprenticed: To learn a trade under a craftsman

aristocracy: The highest class in certain societies

Arminianism: The belief that affirms human free will regarding salvation

asthma: An inflammatory lung

athirst: Being eager, urgent need for something

bade: Asked

bounden: Bound to a promise or principle

brigades: Divisions of the army

Calvinism: The belief that God pre-determines who will be saved

carousing: Enjoying oneself in a noisy, lively way

chambers: Guest rooms

chaplain: Preacher

chink: Fill in spaces between logs

commentaries: Books that help explain the text

converted: Saved

covenant: A spiritual agreement or contract

denominations: A distinct religious body identified by traits such as a common name, structure, leadership, and doctrine.

deplorable: Very bad

deter: Stop

dilapidated: In need of repair

disembarked: Stepped off the train

distraught: Very upset

elements: Bad weather

encapsulates: Expresses the essential features of

encompassed: Included

encumbrances: Burdensome possessions

evangelists: Preachers who often travel to share the gospel

evicted: Forced

expounded: Commented

fervent: Passionate

Flair: Able to do something very well

forbade: Not allowed to do something

forged: Directed

forsook: Something left or abandoned

fundamental: Basic, central

grammar school: School that taught languages and basic math and geography

Great Awakening: A religious revival that impacted the English colonies in America during the 1730s–1740s

headstrong: Stubborn

heathen: One who does not believe in religion

heralded: Advertised

Herr: German word for Mister

hypothermia: When the body loses heat faster than it can produce it, often leading to death.

immersion: Submersion in water

immigrants: Persons who come to live permanently in a foreign country

impoverished: Very poor

indignant: Upset

ingenuity: The skill and imagination to create new things

intrigued: Drawn in

itinerate: Traveling minister

laymen: Non-clergy men who had responsibilities helping with a church

listing: Leaning

Loyalists: Loyal to England and in opposition to independence

maiden: First-ever

marmoset: South American monkey with a long tail

mechanical reaping machine: A horse-drawn machine that revolutionized agriculture

mentor: Advisor

methodically: Systematically

Moravian: A member of the Moravian Church, one of the oldest Christian denominations

mortgage: Payment.

ordained: Officially made

ordination: To be officially recognized as a representative of the Church

parishioners: Church members

pawnbroker: A person who lends money at interest

persevere: Keep on when conditions were hard

pew: Long wooden rows used as seats in church

pickpockets: People who stole from others

pondered: Gave serious and careful thought

pound: A unit of money used in Britain

Providence: Reference to God working in our lives

Prussia: Today's modern Germany

Puritan: English Protestants of the 16th and 17th centuries who sought to purify the existing church

rapt: Captivated

reputable: Well-thought-of

row houses: A row of houses joined together

Sacrament: A religious act done with reverence and obedience

Second Great Awakening: The revival in the United States from about 1795 to 1835 when many people turned to God

seminary: Colleges for preachers

smelting: The extraction of metal from its ore by a process of heating and melting it

spar: Strong pole such as the mast of a ship

stipulations: Conditions he must agree to

succumbed: Died

The Hermitage: The name of Jackson's home

theologian: One who studies and teaches about God

tuberculosis: A disease of the lungs

unfailing: Reliable

wrestle: Deeply considered

yon: A person over there

Zululand: Now known as KwaZulu-Natal province in South Africa

Corresponding Curriculum

Foundations of the Faith Series
Famous Preachers and Evangelist • Book 2

All the stories in this book can correspond with the following Master Books Curriculum:

- *A Child's Geography* (Series)
- *The World's Story* (Series)
- *For You They Signed*
- *American and World History* (Series)
- *History of Religious Liberty*
- *Language Lessons for a Living Education*
- *Timeline of American History*
- *Adam's Chart of History*

Endnotes

1 Wesley & Jackson 1979, Sermon #53: On The Death of The Rev. Mr. George Whitefield.

2 Warren W. Wiersbe, *The Wycliffe Handbook of Preaching and Preachers* (Chicago: Moody Press, 1984).

3. Janet and Geoff Benge, *John Wesley: The World His Parish* (Seattle, Washington: YWAM Publishing, 2007) 22.

4. Basil Miller, *John Wesley* (Minneapolis, Minnesota: Bethany House Publishers, 1943) 28.

5. Ibid. 32.

6. Ibid. 54.

7. Ibid. 61.

8. Benge, *John Wesley: The World His Parish* 105.

9. Ibid. 106.

10. Miller, *John Wesley* 73.

11. Stephen Tomkins, *John Wesley: A Biography* (Grand Rapids, Michigan: Wm B. Eerdmans, 2003) 83.

12. Benge, *John Wesley: The World His Parish* 140.

13. Ibid. 140.

14. Ibid. 168.

15. Tomkins, *John Wesley: A Biography* 192.

16. Benge, *John Wesley: The World His Parish* 188.

17. David Vaughn, *A Divine Light: The Spiritual Leadership of Jonathan Edwards* (Nashville, Tennessee: Cumberland House, 2007) 24.

18. Christian Timothy George, *Jonathan Edwards: America's Genius* (Scotland, UK: Christian Focus Publications, 2008) 19.

19. Ibid. 19.

20. Glenda Faye Mathes and Joel Beeke, *Puritan Heroes* (Grand Rapids, Michigan: Reformation Heritage Books, 2018) 173.

21. Simonetta Carr, *Jonathan Edwards* (Grand Rapids, Michigan: Reformation Heritage Books, 2014).

22. Ibid. 25.

23. Mathes and Beeke, *Puritan Heroes* 175.

24. George, *Jonathan Edwards: America's Genius* 92.

25. Carr, *Jonathan Edwards* 41.

26. Ibid. 41.

27. George, *Jonathan Edwards: America's Genius* 112.

28. Carr, *Jonathan Edwards* 50.

29. Ibid. 54.

30. George, *Jonathan Edwards: America's Genius* 132.

31. Bruce and Becky Durost Fish, *George Whitefield: Pioneering Evangelist* (Barbour Publishing:

Uhrichsville, Ohio, 2000) 19.

32. Ibid. 25.
33. Ibid. 28.
34. Lucille Travis, *George Whitefield: The Voice that Woke the World* (Scotland, UK: Christian Focus Publications, 2011) 23.
35. Ibid. 44.
36. Ibid. 46.
37. Ibid. 51.
38. Ibid. 53.
39. Ibid. 61.
40. Ibid. 69.
41. Ibid. 74.
42. Fish, *George Whitefield: Pioneering Evangelist* 8.
43. Ibid. 9.
44. Travis, *George Whitefield: The Voice that Woke the World* 169–170.
45. Ibid. 171.
46. Janet and Geoff Benge, *Francis Asbury: Circuit Rider* (Seattle, Washington: YWAM Publishing, 2013) 26.
47. Ibid. 30.
48. L. C. Rudolph, *Francis Asbury* (Nashville, Tennessee: Abingdon Press, 1966) 72.
49. Ibid. 82.
50. Benge, *Francis Asbury: Circuit Rider* 85.
51. Ibid. 121.
52. Ibid. 125.
53. Ibid. 151.
54. Ibid. 179.
55. Ibid. 188.
56. Bessie G. Olson, *Peter Cartwright: A Great Circuit Rider* (Des Moines, Iowa: Boone Publishing Company, 1945) 8.
57. Nancy Veglahn, *Peter Cartwright: Pioneer Circuit Rider* (New York: Charles Scribner's Sons, 1968) 14.
58. Ibid. 15.
59. Olson, *Peter Cartwright: A Great Circuit Rider* 9.
60. Ibid. 11.
61. Ibid. 12.
62. Veglahn, *Peter Cartwright: Pioneer Circuit Rider* 72.
63. Ibid. 88.
64. Olson, *Peter Cartwright: A Great Circuit Rider* 33.
65. Veglahn, *Peter Cartwright: Pioneer Circuit Rider* 187.
66. Faith Coxe Bailey, *George Mueller: He Dared to Trust God for the Needs of Countless Orphans* (Chicago, Illinois: Moody Press, 1958) 127.
67. Janet and Geoff Benge, *George Mueller: The Guardian of Bristol Orphans* (Seattle, Washington: YWAM Publishing, 1999) 167–168.
68. Ibid. 158.
69. Ibid. 171.
70. Simonetta Carr, *Charles Haddon Spurgeon* (Grand Rapids, Michigan: Reformation Heritage

Books, 2021) 55.

71. Joel R. Beeke and Douglas Bond, *Evangelical Heroes Volume 2* (Grand Rapids, Michigan: Reformation Heritage Books, 2023) 15.
72. Carr, *Charles Haddon Spurgeon* 14.
73. Ibid. 15.
74. Beeke and Bond, *Evangelical Heroes Volume 2* 14.
75. Ibid. 19.
76. Carr, *Charles Haddon Spurgeon* 36.
77. Ibid. 44.
78. Ibid. 54.
79. Christian Timothy George, *Charles Spurgeon: The Prince of Preachers* (Scotland, UK: Christian Focus Publications, 2006) 145.
80. Ibid. 9.
81. Janet and Geoff Benge, *William Booth: Soup, Soap, and Salvation* (Seattle, Washington: YWAM Publishing, 2002) 191.
82. Helen Hosier, *William and Catherine Booth: Founders of the Salvation Army* (Uhrichsville, Ohio: Barbour Publishing, 1999) 14.
83. Ibid. 16-17.
84. Benge, *William Booth: Soup, Soap, and Salvation* 33.
85. Ibid. 71.
86. Ibid. 76.
87. Hosier, *William and Catherine Booth: Founders of the Salvation Army* 88.
88. Ibid. 159.
89. Ibid. 202.
90. Janet and Geoff Benge, *D.L. Moody: Bringing Souls to Christ* (Seattle, Washington: YWAM Publishing, 2021) 30-31.
91. Faith Coxe Bailey, *D.L. Moody: The Greatest Evangelist of the Nineteenth Century* (Chicago, Illinois: Moody Publishers, 1959) 22.
92. Bonnie C. Harvey, *D.L. Moody: The American Evangelist* (Uhrichsville, Ohio: Barbour Publishing, 1997) 35.
93. Benge, *D.L. Moody: Bringing Souls to Christ* 59.
94. Nancy Drummond, *D.L. Moody: One Devoted Man* (Scotland, UK: Christian Focus Publications, 2015) 30.
95. Benge, *D.L. Moody: Bringing Souls to Christ* 66.
96. Ibid. 67.
97. Drummond, *D.L. Moody: One Devoted Man* 61.
98. Harvey, *D.L. Moody: The American Evangelist* 123.
99. Ibid. 137.
100. Benge, *D.L. Moody: Bringing Souls to Christ* 160.
101. Ibid. 189.
102. Moody Adams, *The Titanic's Last Hero* (Columbia, South Carolina: The Olive Press, 1997) 48.
103. Ibid. 28–29.
104. Ibid. 37.
105. Ibid. 39.
106. Ibid. 43.
107. Logan Marshall, *The Sinking of the Titanic and Great Sea Disasters* (Orinda, California: Sea Wolf Press, 2021) 4.

108. Ibid. 4.
109. Adams, *The Titanic's Last Hero* 15.
110. Ibid. 41.
111. Marshall, *The Sinking of the Titanic and Great Sea Disasters* 13.
112. Ibid. 22.
113. Ibid. 27.
114. Ibid. 28.
115. Victor Maxwell, *Titanic: John Harper-God's Man Behind the Legend* (UK: Biblical Books, 2012) 33.